Merrickville Ontario in Colour Photos, Saving Our History One Photo at a Time

Photography
by Barbara Raué
2016

Series Name:
Cruising Ontario

Book 158: Merrickville

Cover photo: 206 Main Street East, Page 41

Series Name: Cruising Ontario
Saving Our History One Photo at a Time
in colour photos

Books Available in Alphabetical Order:
Aberfoyle, Acton, Alton, Amherstburg, Ancaster, Arthur, Aylmer, Ayr, Bloomingdale, Brantford, Burlington, Caledon, Caledonia, Cambridge, Clifford, Conestogo, Delhi, Dorchester to Aylmer, Drayton, Drumbo, Dundas, Eden Mills, Elmira, Elora, Essex, Fergus, Guelph, Hagersville, Hamilton, Hanover, Harriston, Hespeler, Jarvis, Kingston, Kingsville, Kitchener, Linwood, Listowel, London, Lucknow, Mono, Mount Forest, Neustadt, New Hamburg, Niagara-on-the-Lake, Oakville, Orangeville, Orillia, Owen Sound, Palmerston, Peterborough, Petrolia, Port Elgin, Preston, Rockwood, Sarnia, Seaforth, Sheffield, Shelburne, Simcoe, Southampton, St. Jacobs, St. Marys, St. Thomas, Stoney Creek, Stratford, Thamesford, Tillsonburg, Waterdown, Waterford, Waterloo, Welland, Wellesley, Windsor, Wingham, Woodstock

Book 125-127: Woodstock
Book 128: Thamesford
Book 129-132: St. Marys
Book 133-136: Sarnia
Book 137: Petrolia
Book 138-139: Welland
Book 140-145: Kingston
Book 146-149: Ottawa
Book 150-151: Midland
Book 152: Penetanguishene
Book 153: Kemptville
Book 154: Cornwall
Book 155: Mariatown to Maitland

Book 156: Morrisburg
Book 157: Brockville
Book 158: Merrickville
Book 159: Smiths Falls
Book 160: Portland, Newboro
Book 161: Westport & Area
Book 162: Perth

Other Books by Barbara Raue

Coins of Gold

Arrows, Indians and Love

The Life and Times of Barbara
Volume 1: Inventions That Have Enhanced My Life
Volume 2: Entertainment That I Have Enjoyed
Volume 3: East Coast Trips
Volume 4: Olympics Have Always Intrigued Me
Volume 5: Wonders of the World
Volume 6: Caribbean Cruises We Have Enjoyed
Volume 7: Animals
Volume 8: Storms and Other Major Disasters in My Lifetime
Volume 9: Wars, Terrorist Attacks and Major Disasters

The Cromwell Family Book

Laura Secord Discovered

Daddy Where Are You?

Montana Series
Book 1: Montana Dream
Book 2: Life on the Montana Frontier
Book 3: Montana to Boston and Back

Visit Barbara's website to view all of her books
http://barbararaue.ca

Table of Contents

St. Lawrence Street   Page 6

Main Street West   Page 32

Main Street East   Page 40

Church Street   Page 44

Mill Street   Page 45

Brock Street   Page 48

Wellington Street East   Page 53

Elgin Street   Page 54

Drummond Street East   Page 60

Colborne Street East   Page 61

Lewis Street East   Page 63

St. John Street   Page 68

Merrickville Ruins Interpretive Center Page 71

Architectural Terms   Page 73

Building Styles   Page 77

The United Empire Loyalists were the first non-aboriginal people to settle in the Merrickville area. Beginning in 1783, they were forced to leave the United States after the British defeat in the American War of Independence. Most of these settlers were farmers of Welsh, German, Dutch, Scottish and Irish descent. By settling along the Rideau River, they had access to rich soil, a source of fresh water, and a communication lifeline as the river could keep them connected to each other and to other communities along its banks. In 1793, William Merrick acquired a saw mill from Roger Stevens at the "Great Falls" on the Rideau River (there was a drop of fourteen feet in the river), and then began building new mills which formed the nucleus of Merricks Mills.

As industry grew, farms provided the mills with resources to process. Lumber, corn, oats, wheat, hides, and wool kept the mills running and ensured the region's growing prosperity. Transporting agricultural goods and raw materials such as pig iron became even easier with the construction of the Rideau Canal. From the 1850s to the 1890s, Merrickville was a very important manufacturing center along the Rideau corridor.

Wheels and tools to cut, saw, seed, cultivate, harvest and store agricultural crops were very important. In the 1850s Merrickville leached wood ashes and evaporated the liquid to make potash; they produced twenty barrels, each weighing five hundred pounds, in a year. Potash was used in fertilizers, soaps and other manufactured goods. A cooperage in Merrickville was established in 1845; coopers produced butter churns, tubs, and barrels (for flour, salt pork, etc.). Several brickyards offered an alternative to wood and stone for building materials. Several tanneries were located here; they produced leather from animal skins.

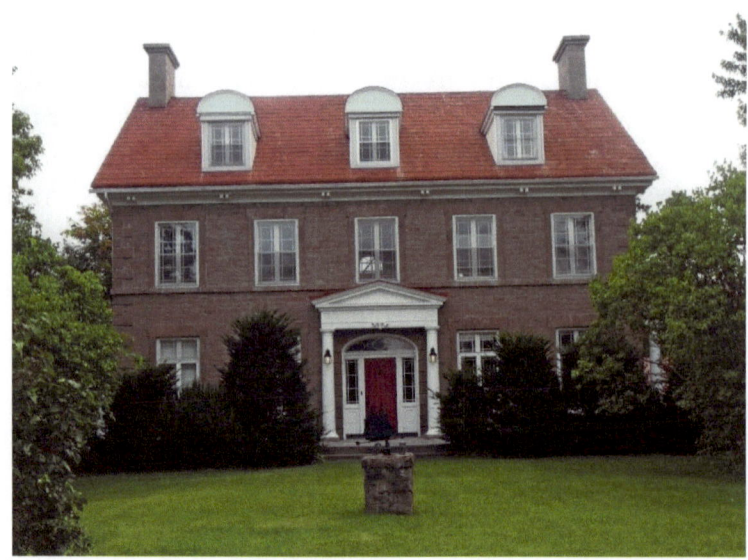

905 St. Lawrence Street - The Aaron Merrick House – built in 1844 of local stone with refined stone window surrounds and oversized stone quoins for the son of the founder of Merrick's Mills – Georgian style with distinct Neo-classical detailing; dormers; semi-elliptical fanlight with sidelights frame a door found within a pedimented portico that is light and elegant

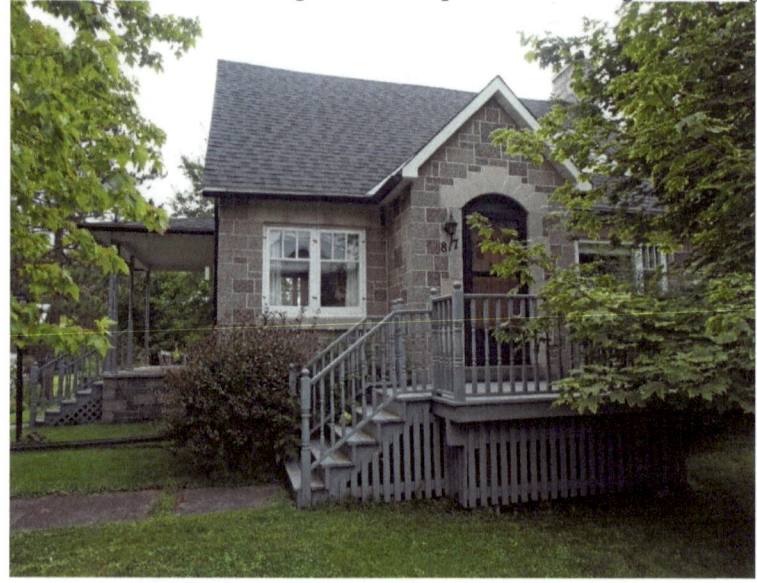

817 St. Lawrence Street – Gothic - stone

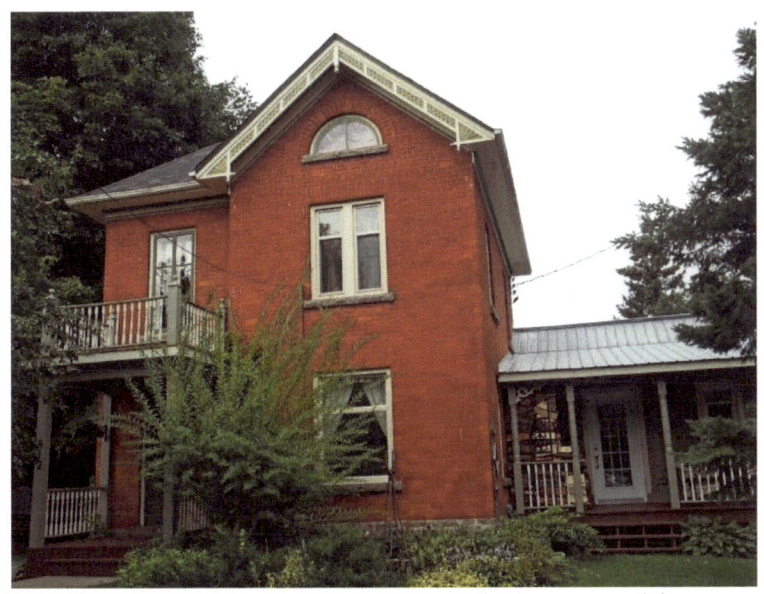

812 St. Lawrence Street – verge board trim on gable, second floor balcony

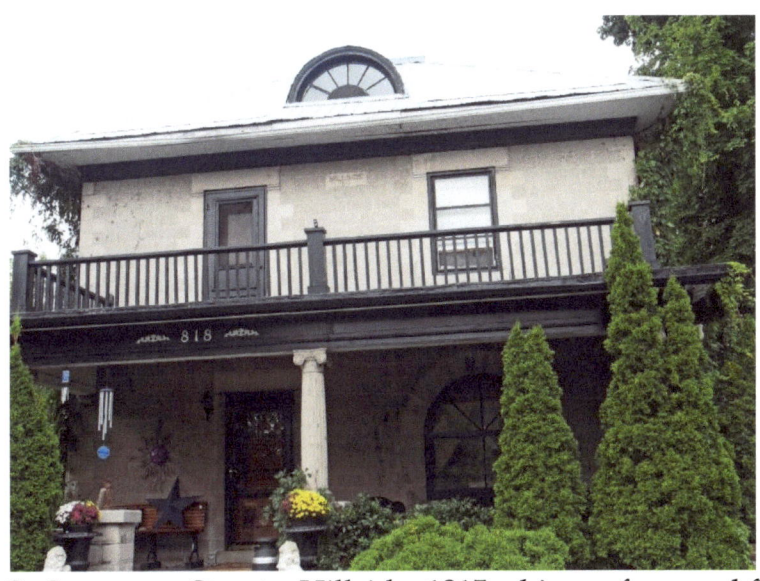

818 St. Lawrence Street – Hillside, 1815 – hip roof, second floor balcony, Ionic capitals for balcony supports

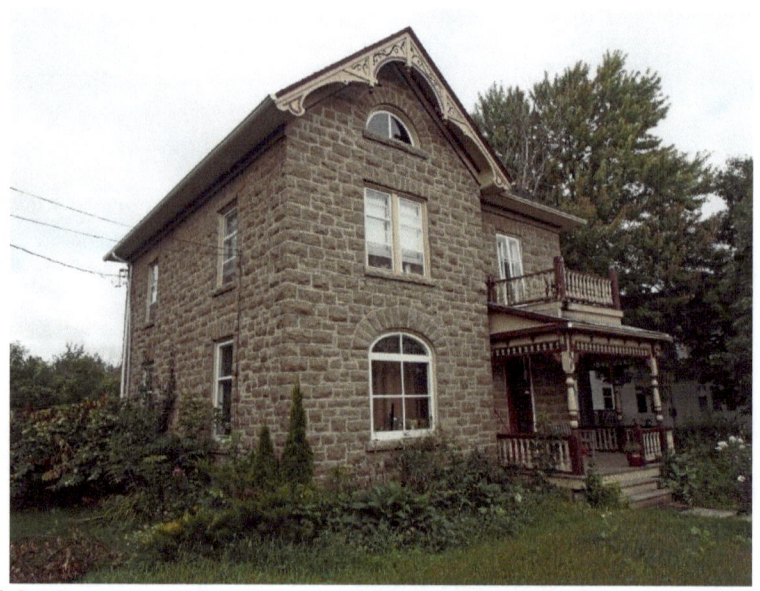

806 St. Lawrence Street – Gothic, verge board trim, decorative wood-turned spindles supporting second floor balcony

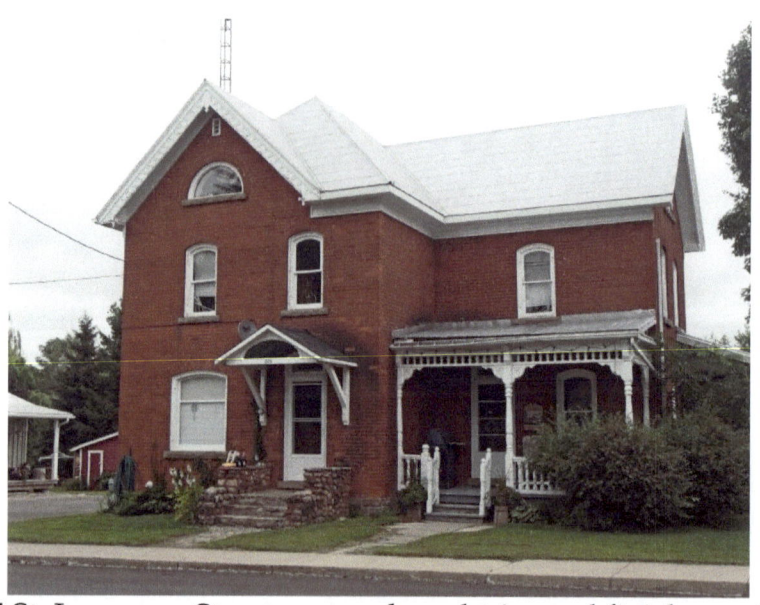

805 St. Lawrence Street – verge board trim and finial on gable

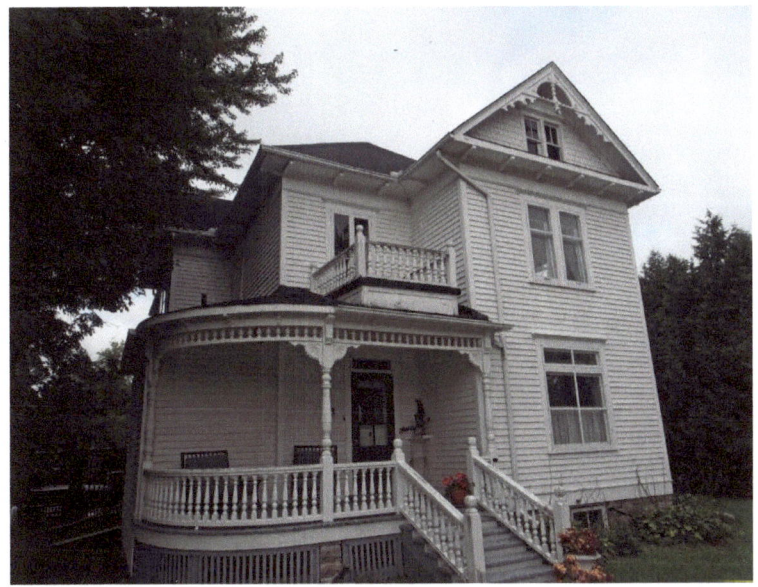

808 St. Lawrence Street – within the peak of the gable is a decorative arch with spindles; second floor balcony; turned veranda roof supports with delicate spindles, open railing

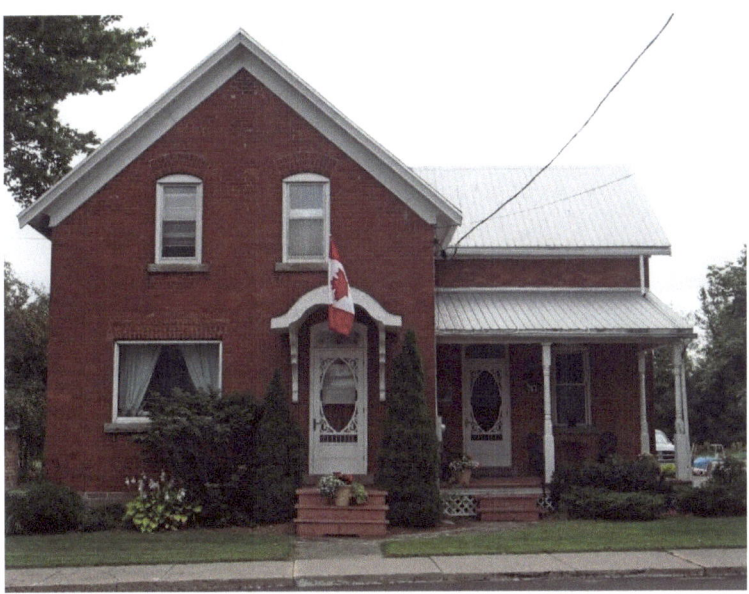

717 St. Lawrence Street – turned veranda roof supports with delicate spindles

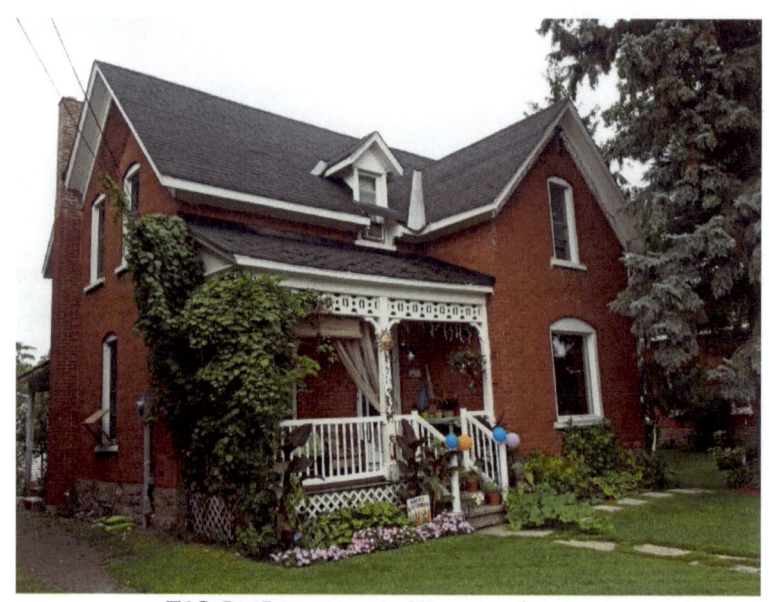
712 St. Lawrence Street - dormer

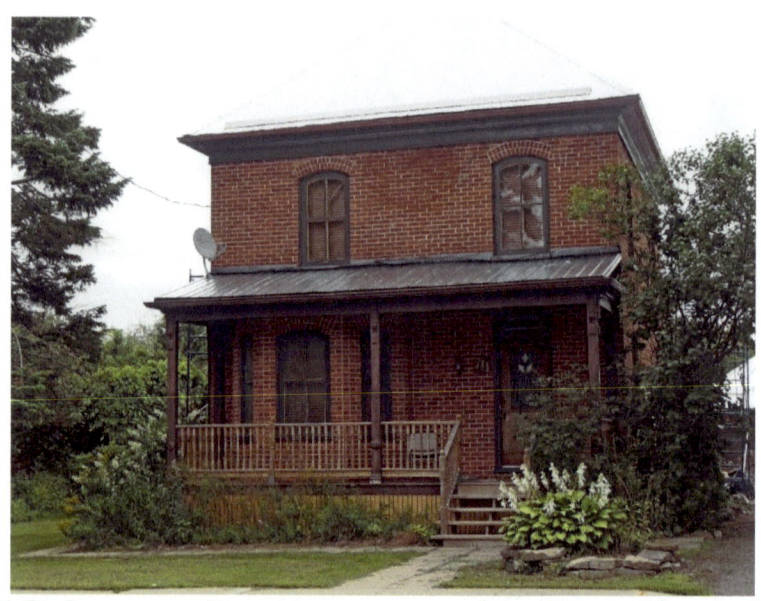
711 St. Lawrence Street – open veranda railing with spindles

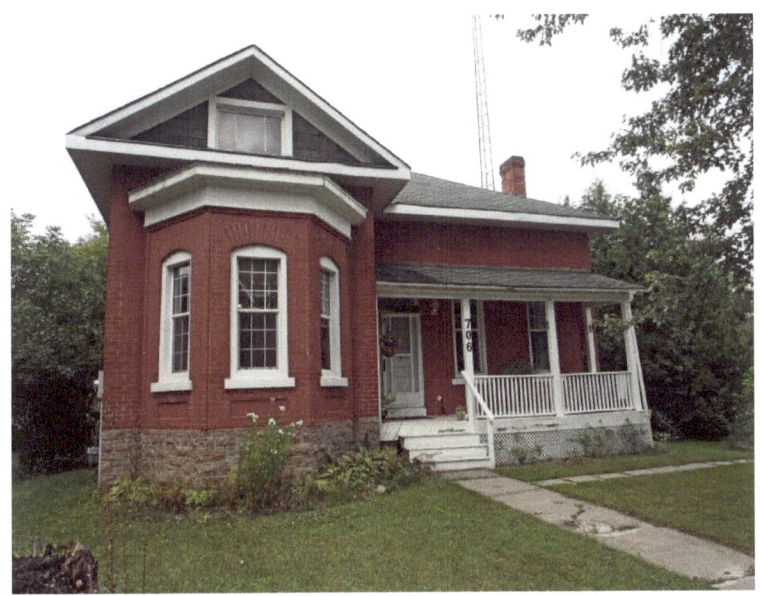

706 St. Lawrence Street – bay window

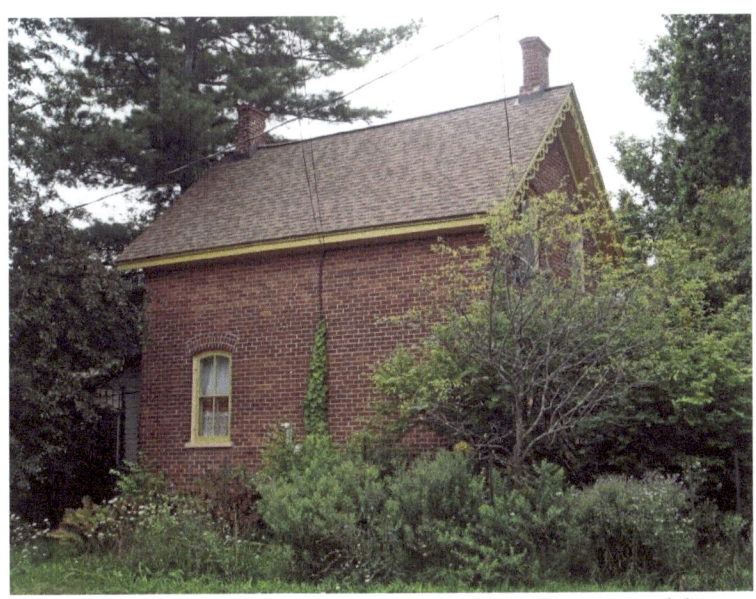

St. Lawrence Street – verge board trim on gable

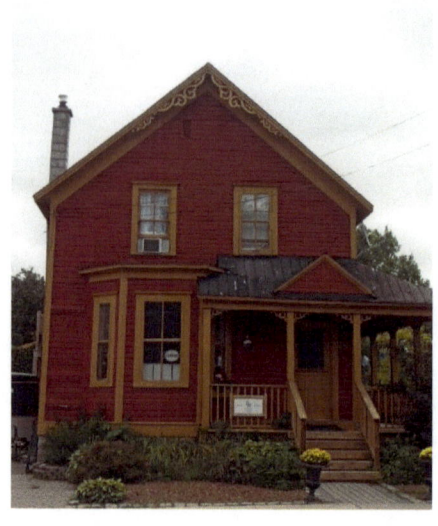

635 Bruce Street - verge board trim on gable, bric-a-brac on top of pillars supporting veranda roof, open railing

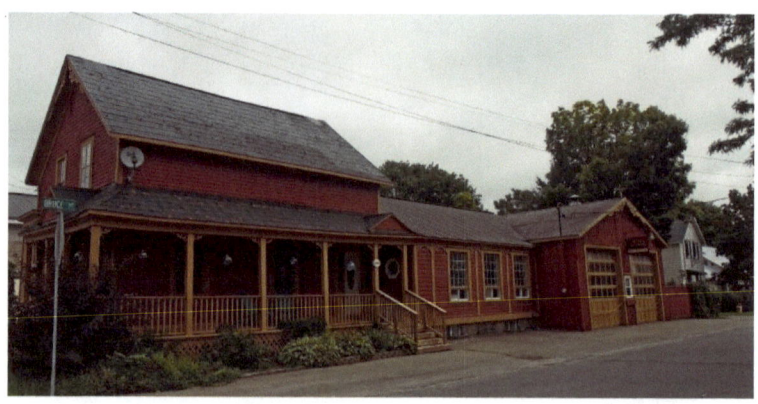

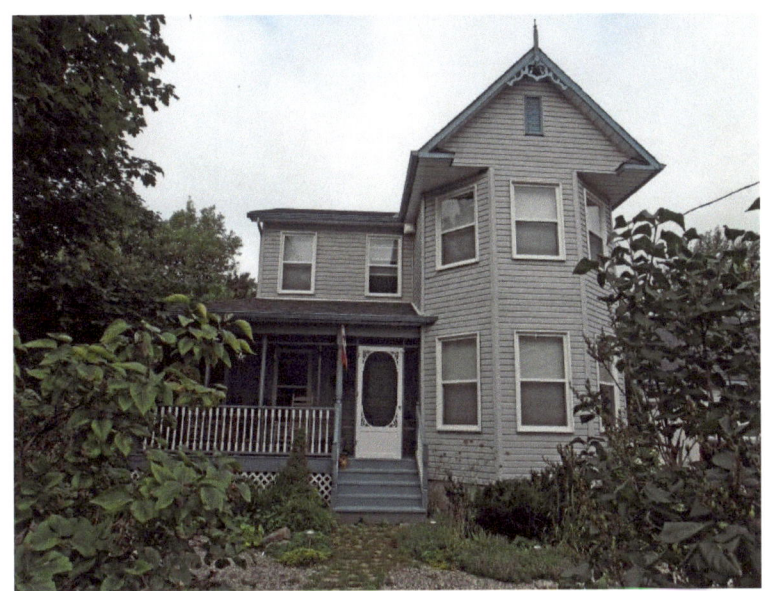

Verge board trim and finial on gable, cornice return, 2½ storey tower-like bay

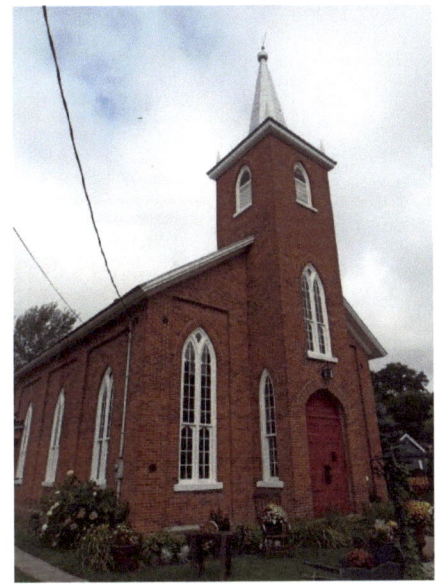

618 St. Lawrence Street
Knox Presbyterian Church
c. 1861 – Gothic Revival
lancet windows

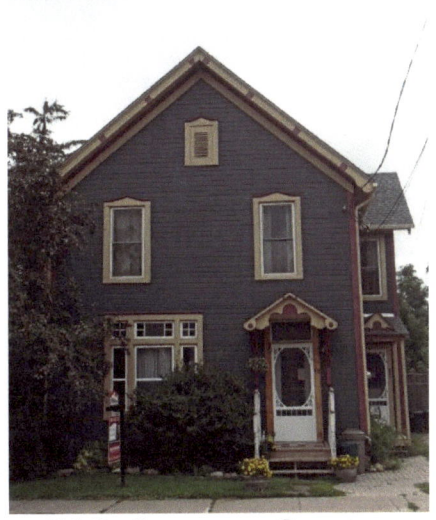

611 St. Lawrence Street

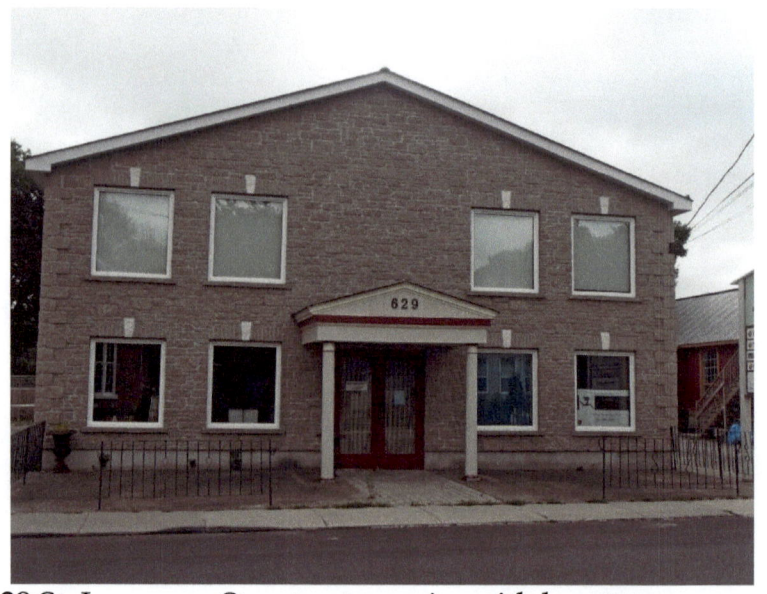

629 St. Lawrence Street – voussoirs with keystones, corner quoins

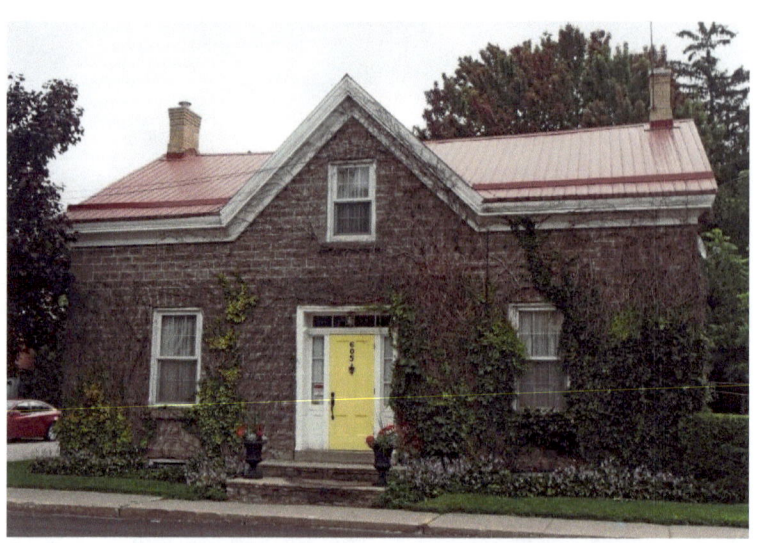

605 St. Lawrence Street – Daniel McEntyre House (shoemaker) – c. 1861 – Gothic Revival – sidelights, transom

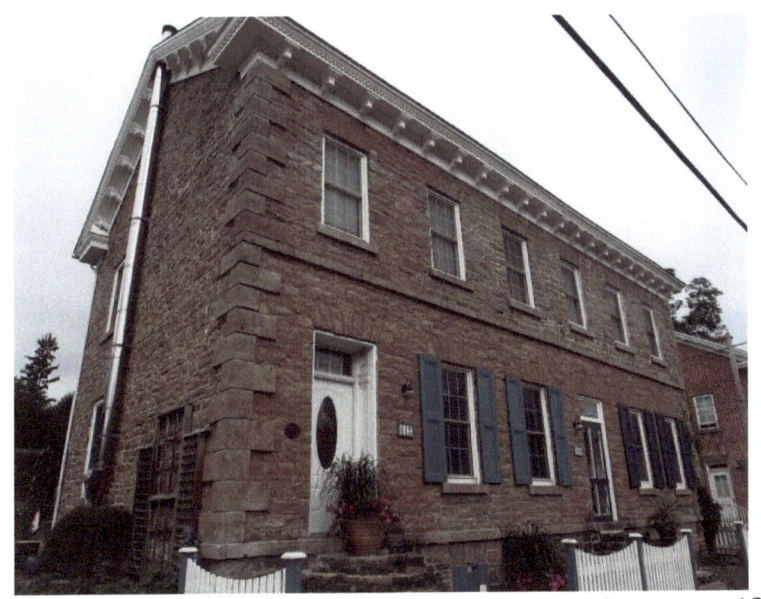

612-606 St. Lawrence Street - Samuel Pearson House – c. 1866
Corner quoins, string course, 6-over-6 sash windows

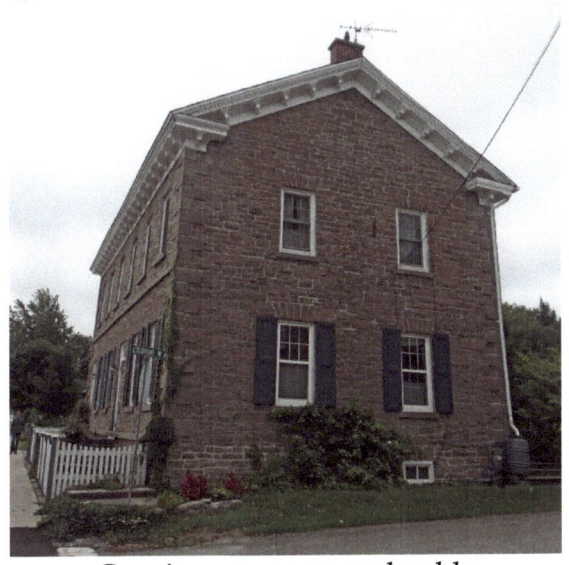

Cornice return on end gable

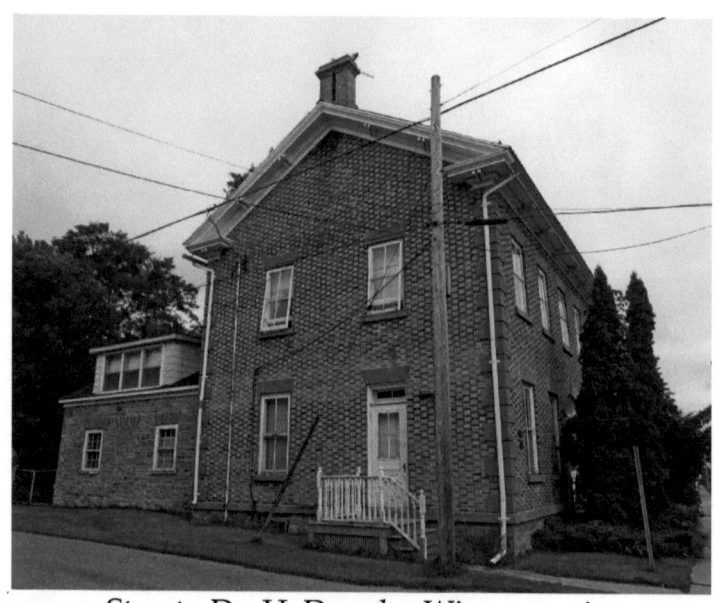

Lawrence Street - Dr. H. Douglas Wise – cornice return on gable, corner quoin

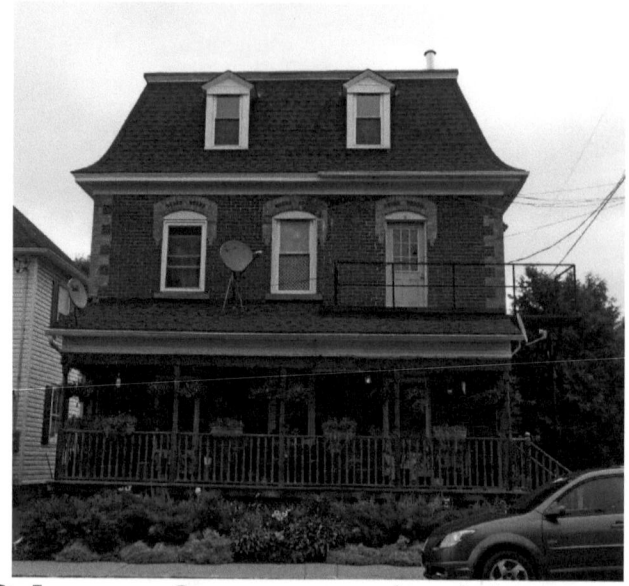

529 St. Lawrence Street – mansard roof, dormers, corner quoins, voussoirs

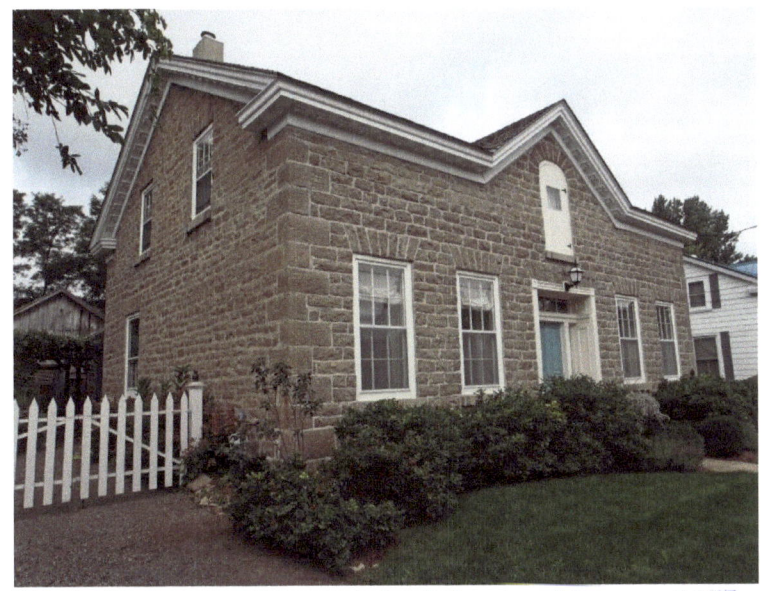

512 St. Lawrence Street - John Johnston House – 1855 – Merrickville Lockmaster (1837-1869 – Gothic Revival - voussoirs, suicide door with no balcony, cornice return on end gable

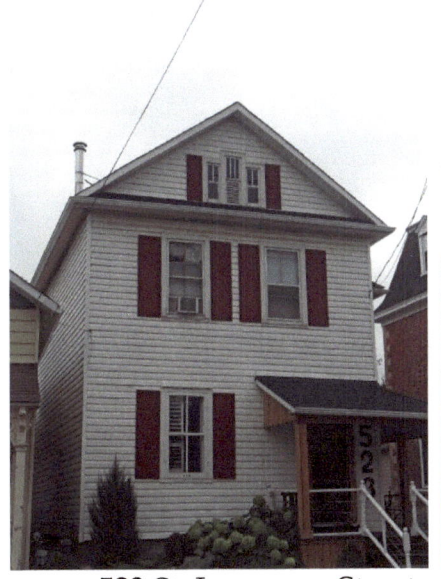

523 St. Lawrence Street Edwardian, Palladian window

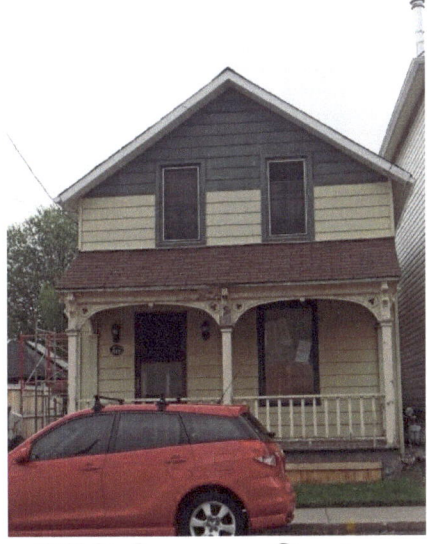

517 St. Lawrence Street

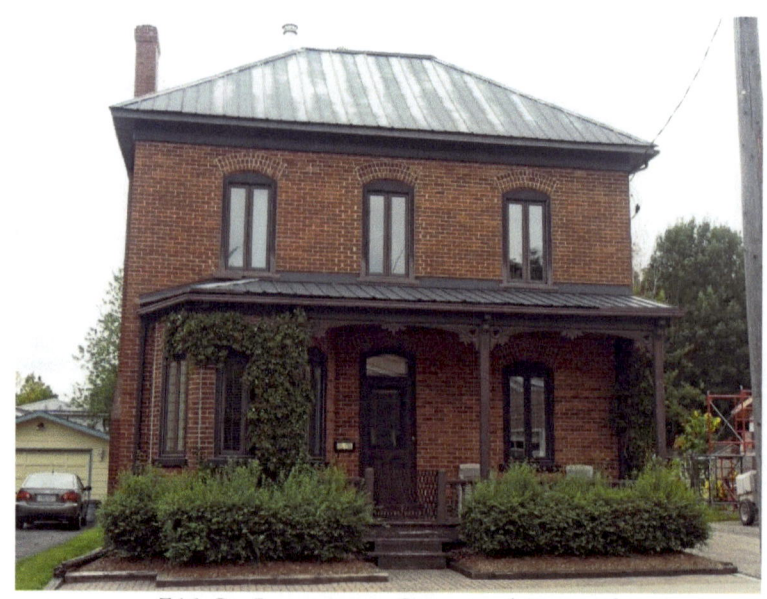

511 St. Lawrence Street – hip roof

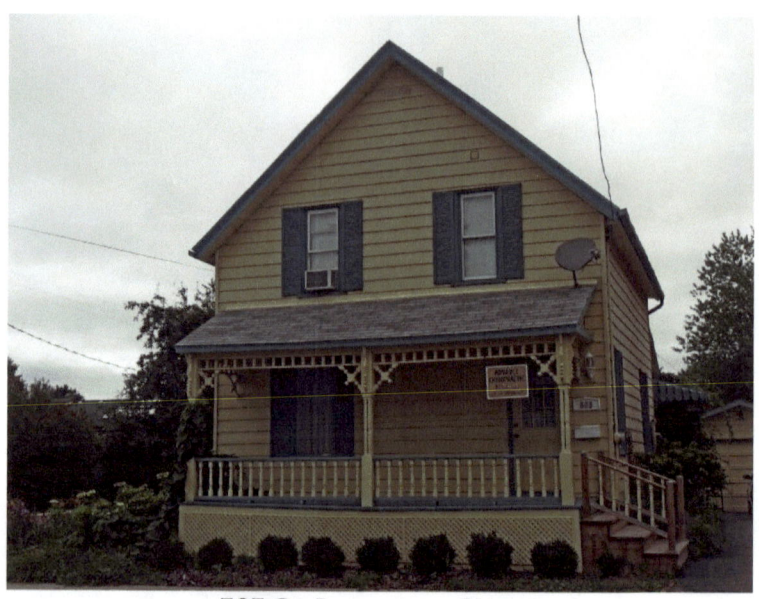

505 St. Lawrence Street

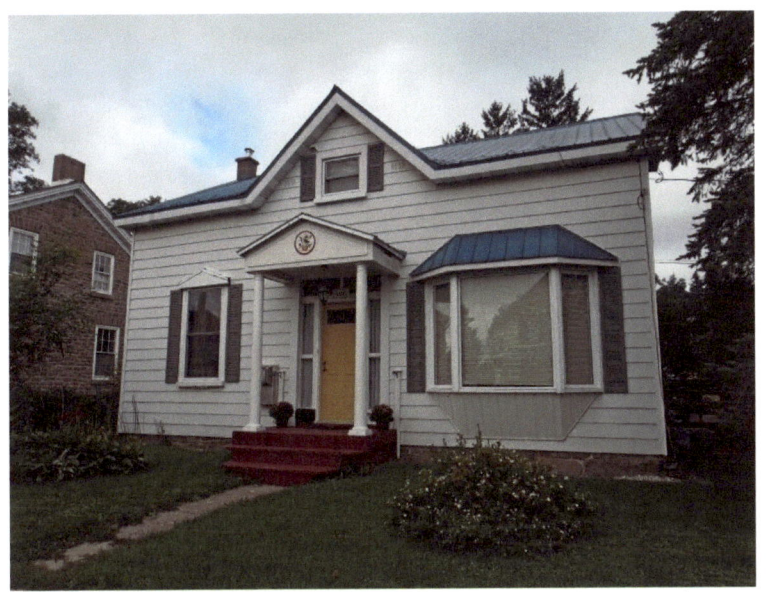

506 St. Lawrence Street – Gothic, bay window, pediment

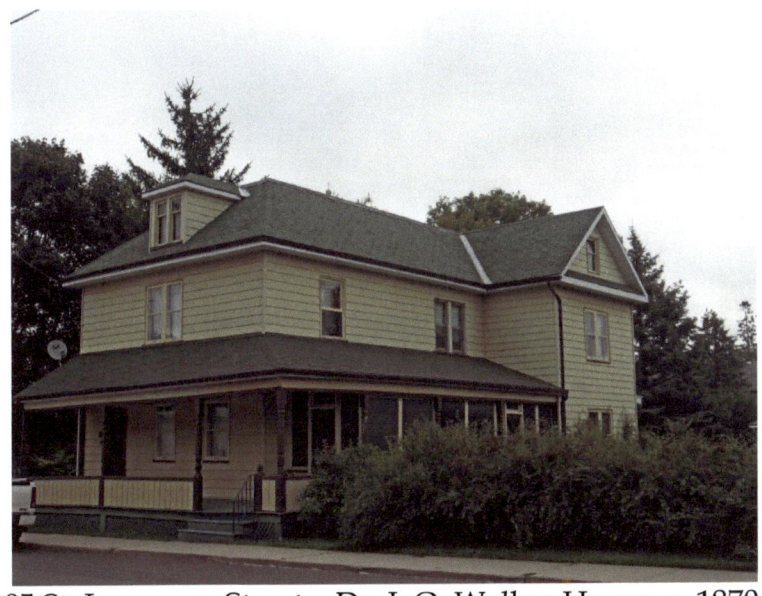

405 St. Lawrence Street – Dr. J. O. Walker House, c. 1870 –
Family Physician (1912-1946) – hip roof, dormer

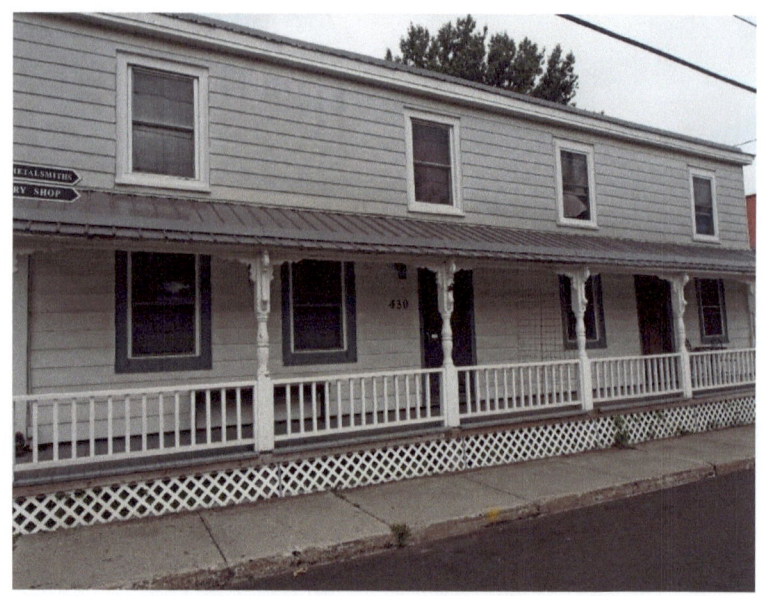

430 St. Lawrence Street – turned veranda roof supports with delicate spindles with decorative capitals

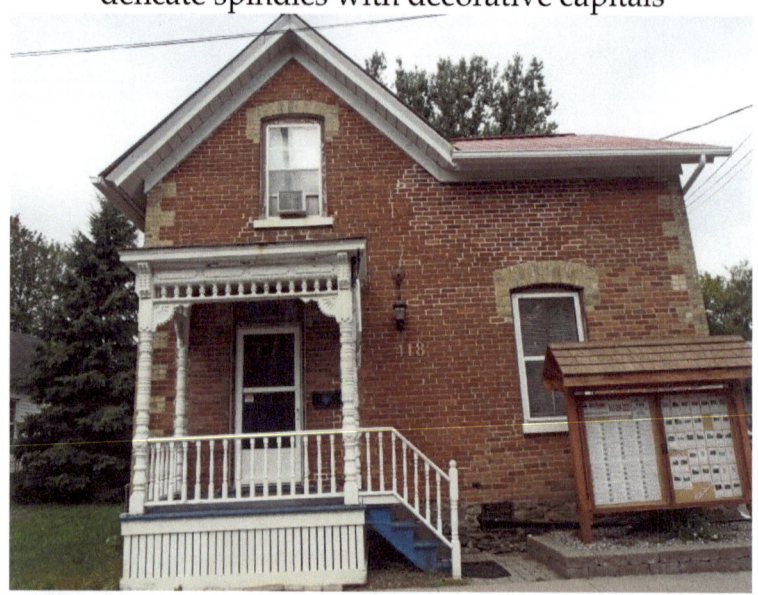

418 St. Lawrence Street – Gothic - turned porch supports with delicate spindles and decorative capitals, dichromatic quoins and voussoirs

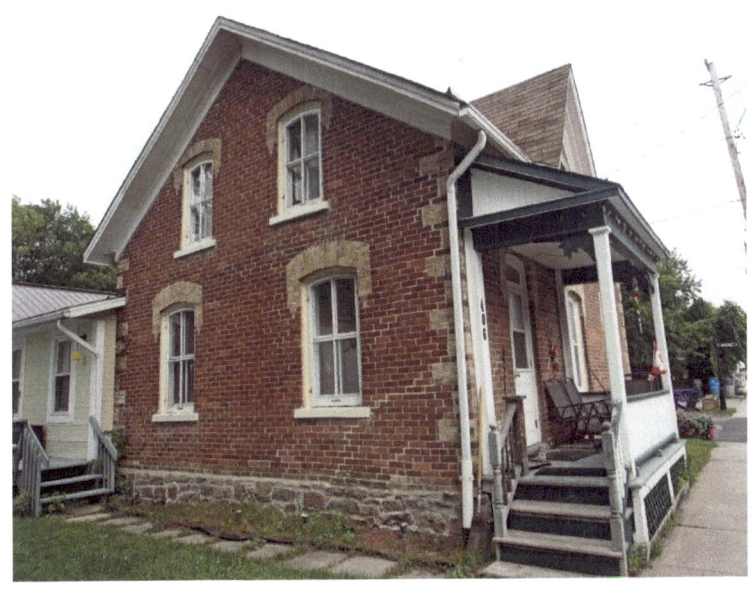

406 St. Lawrence Street – Gothic - dichromatic quoins and voussoirs, cobblestone basement

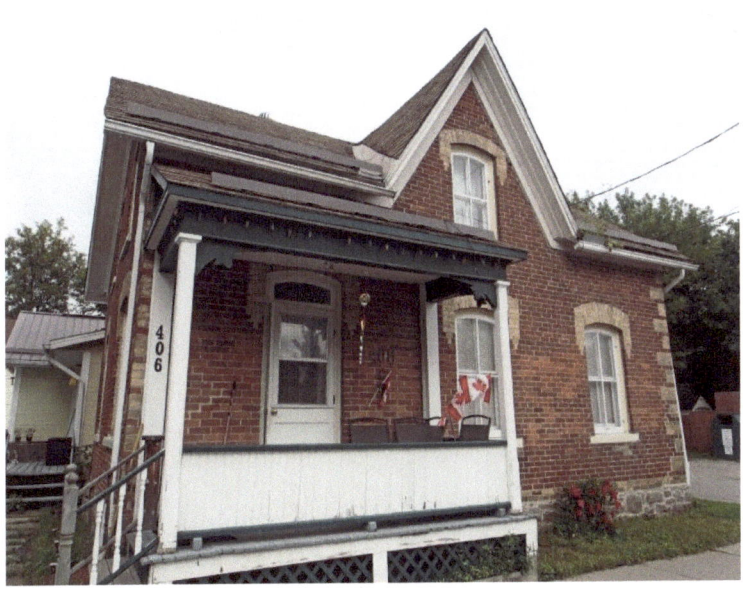

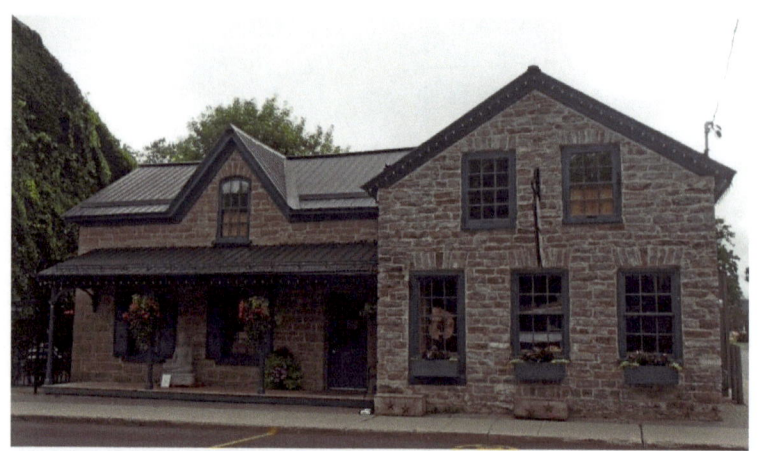

323 St. Lawrence Street – early rubble stone house – c. 1830 - Gothic - voussoirs, 6-over-6 sash windows

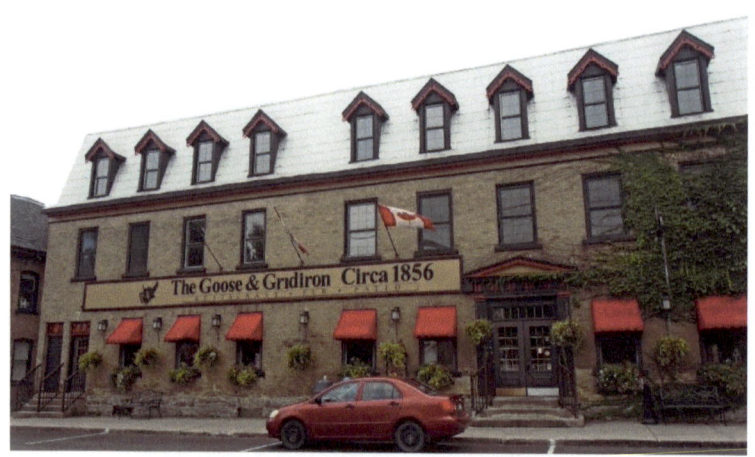

317 St. Lawrence Street – The Goose & Gridiron Restaurant – c. 1856 – Second Empire style – mansard roof, dormers, 6-over-6 sash windows

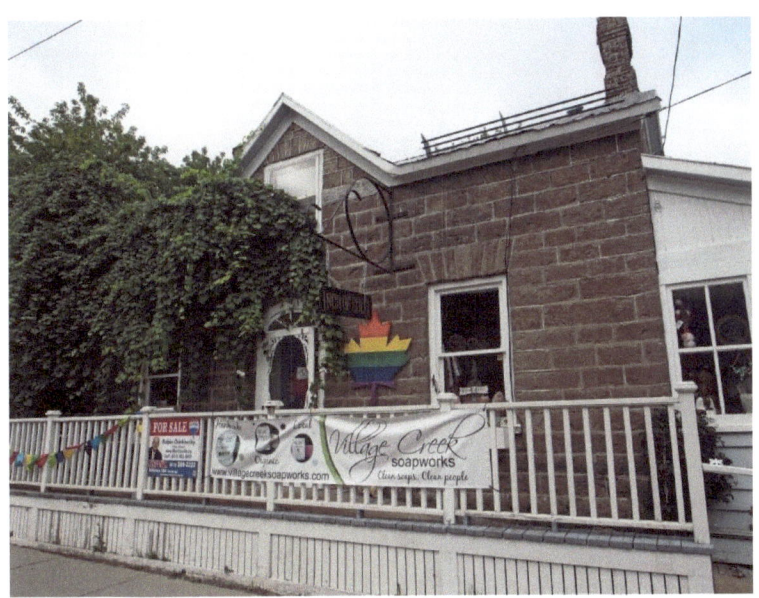

318 St. Lawrence Street – Gothic – stone, voussoirs

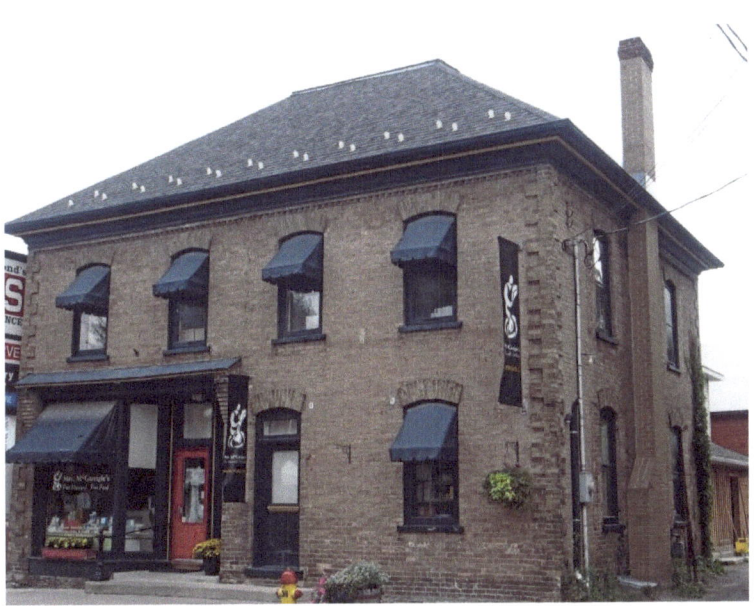

311 St. Lawrence Street – hip roof, saw tooth molding, corner quoins

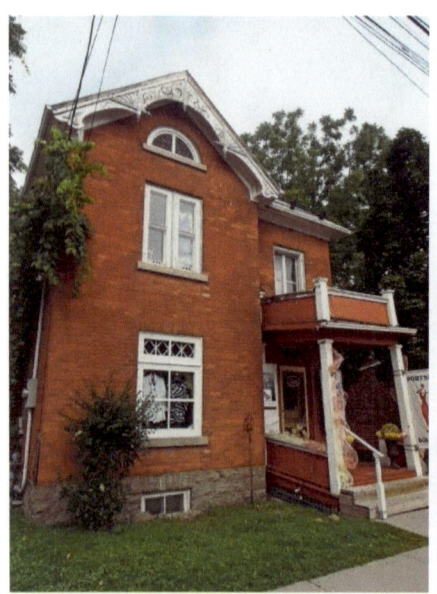

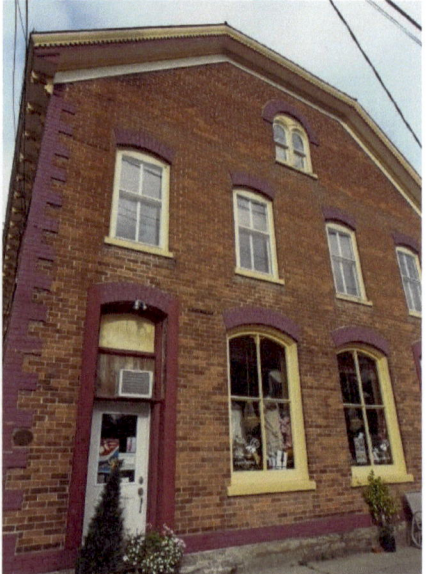

312 St. Lawrence Street   242 St. Lawrence Street
Verge board trim with stenciling   - voussoirs
2nd floor balcony

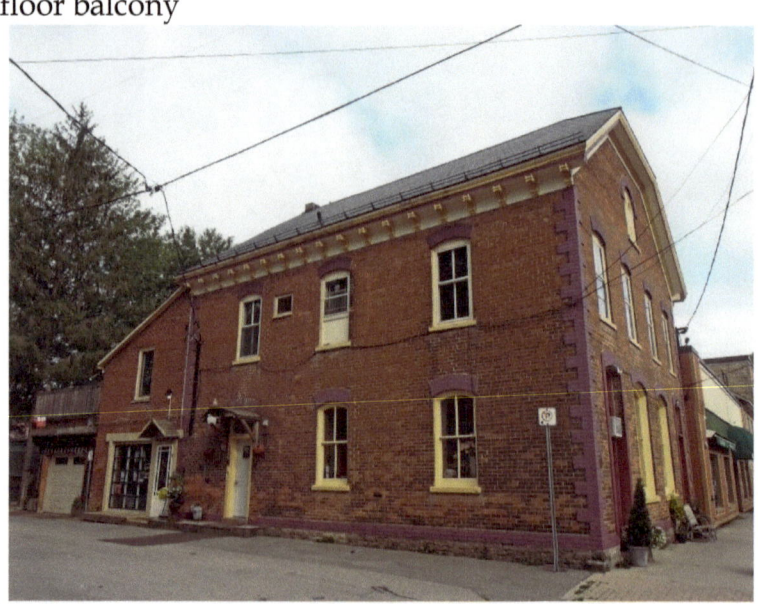

242 St. Lawrence Street – John Mills' Furniture Showroom and
Funeral Home – c. 1868 – operated until the 1930s – corner quoins,
cornice brackets

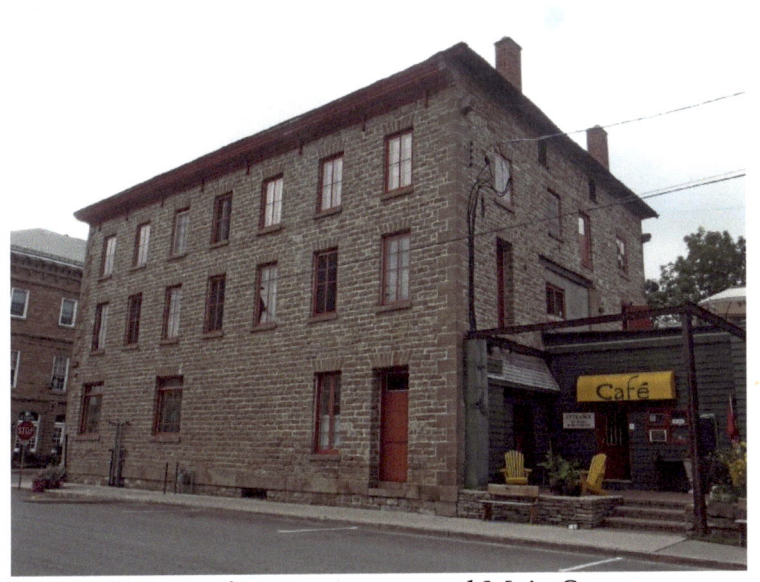

Corner of St. Lawrence and Main Streets

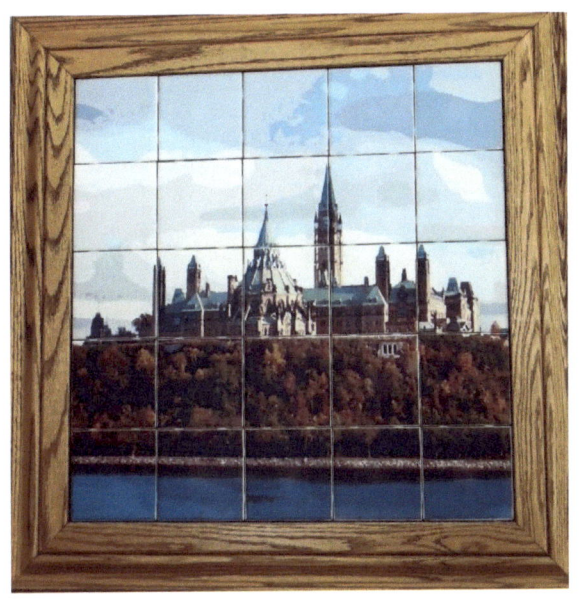

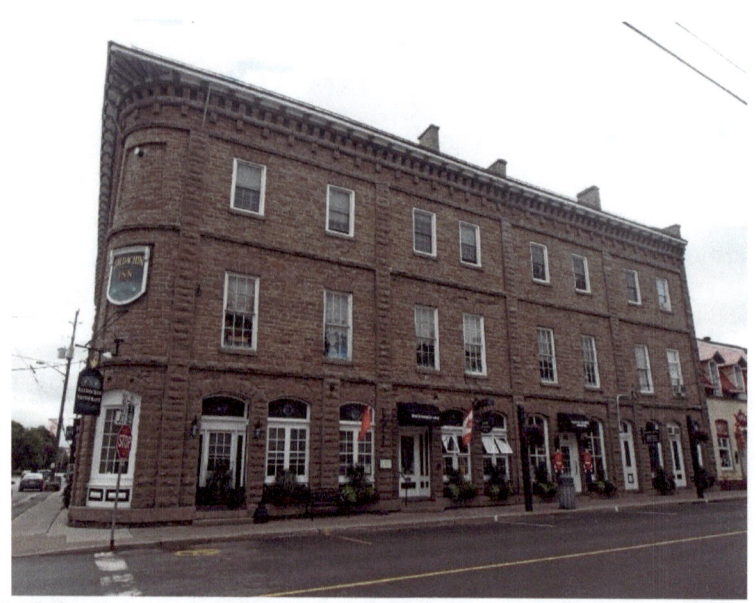

111 St. Lawrence Street – Jakes-McLean Block – c. 1862 – Baldachin Inn and Restaurant - dentil molding, pilasters, string courses, voussoirs

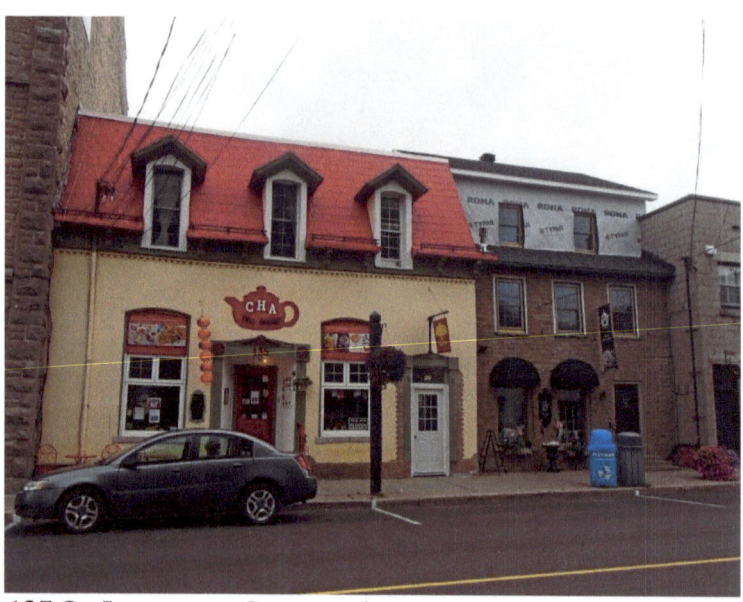

135 St. Lawrence Street – dormers, saw tooth molding

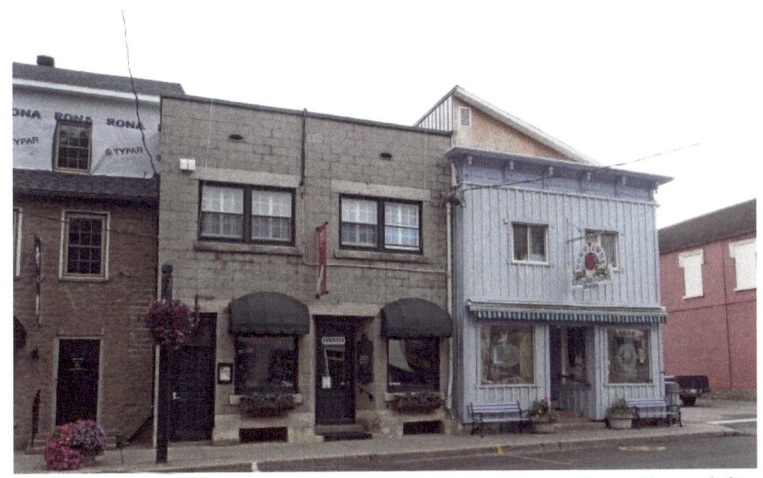

165 St. Lawrence Street – cornice brackets, dentil molding

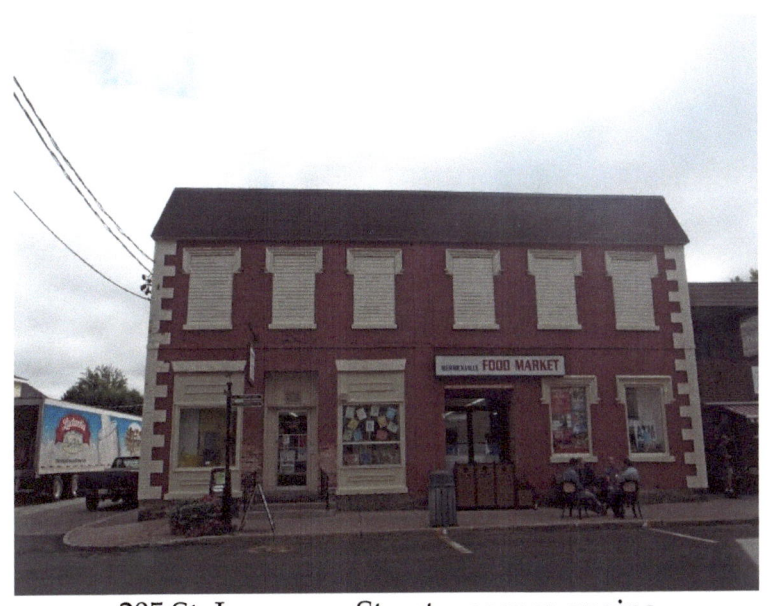

205 St. Lawrence Street – corner quoins

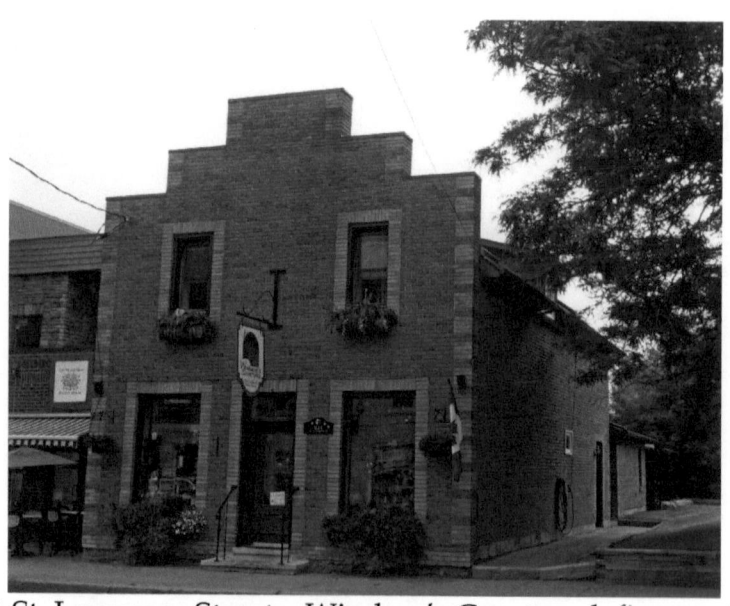

211 St. Lawrence Street – Windsor's Courtyard, fine garden and home décor – dichromatic brickwork, Jacobean gable

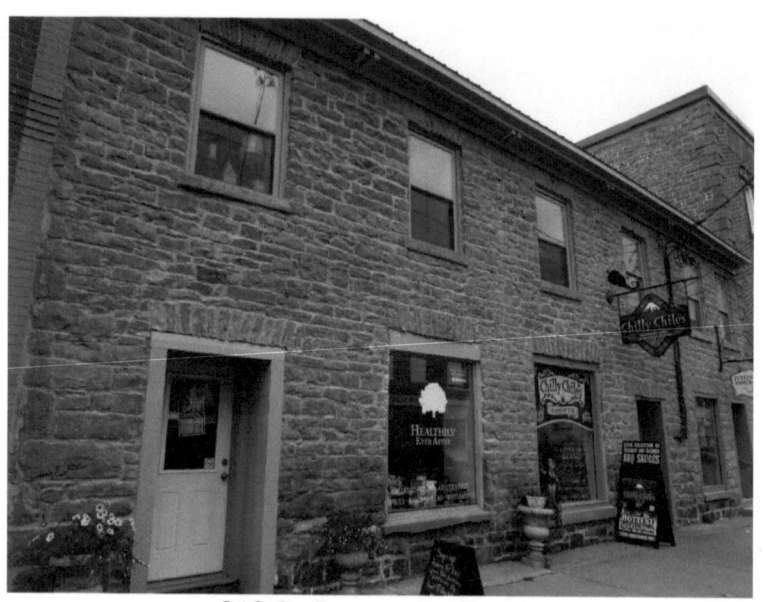

218 St. Lawrence Street

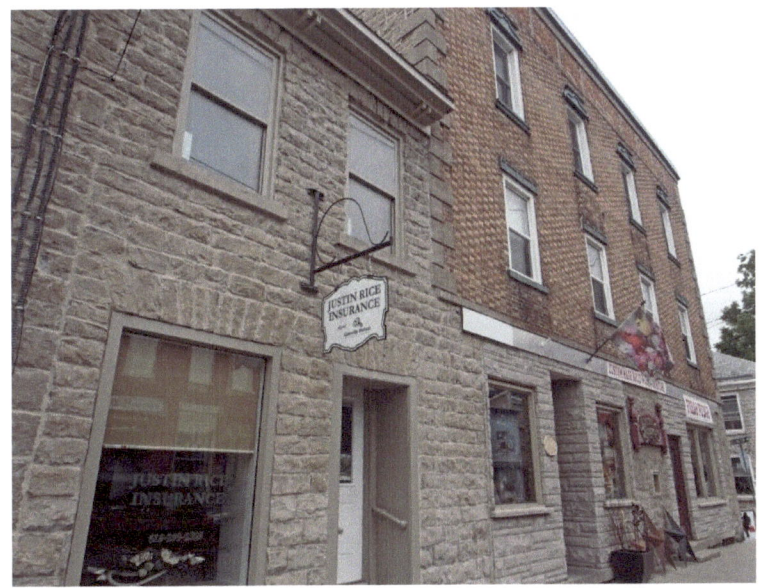

St. Lawrence Street

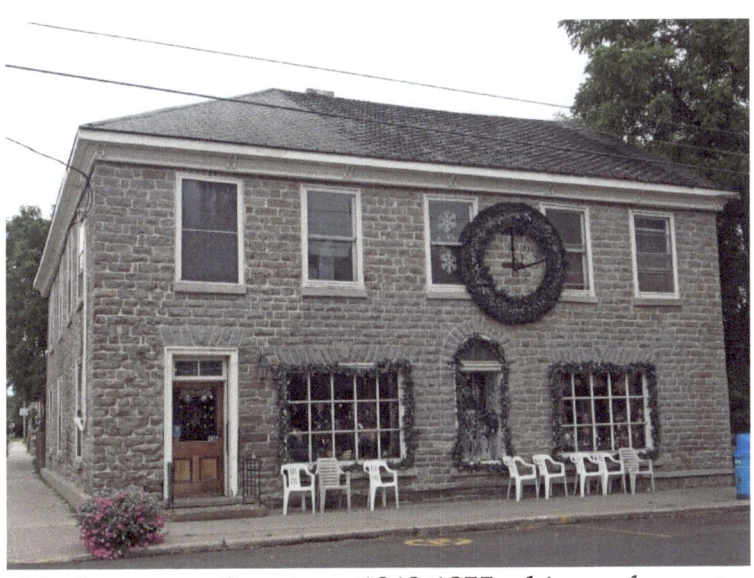

136 St. Lawrence Street – c. 1848-1855 – hip roof, cut stone

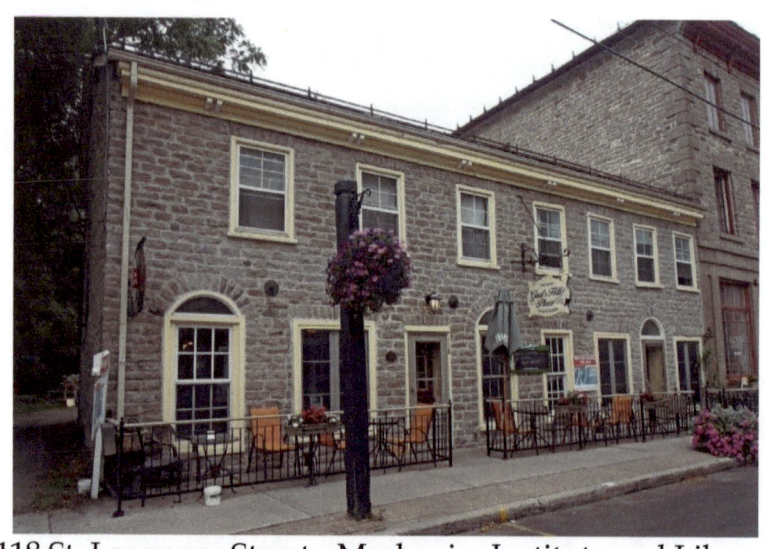

118 St. Lawrence Street - Mechanics Institute and Library Association – c. 1830-1840

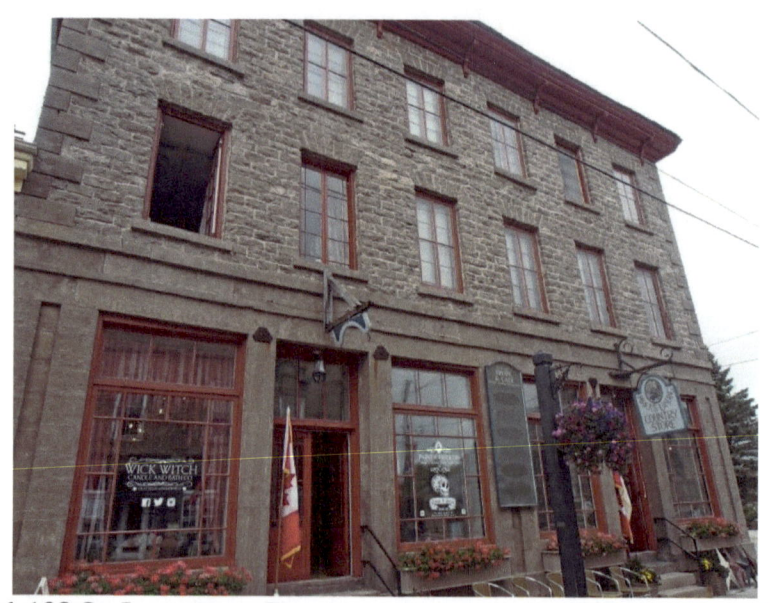

106-108 St. Lawrence Street – Aaron Merrick Block – c. 1856 - stone – voussoirs, cornice brackets

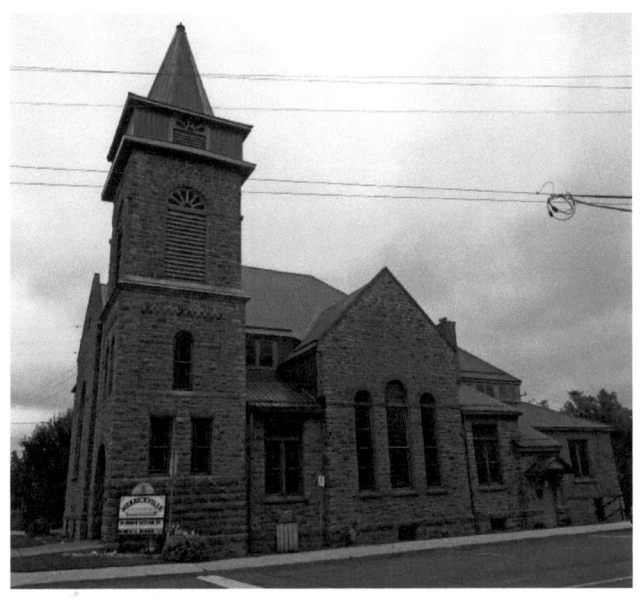

100 St. Lawrence Street - Merrickville United Church
Romanesque – rose window

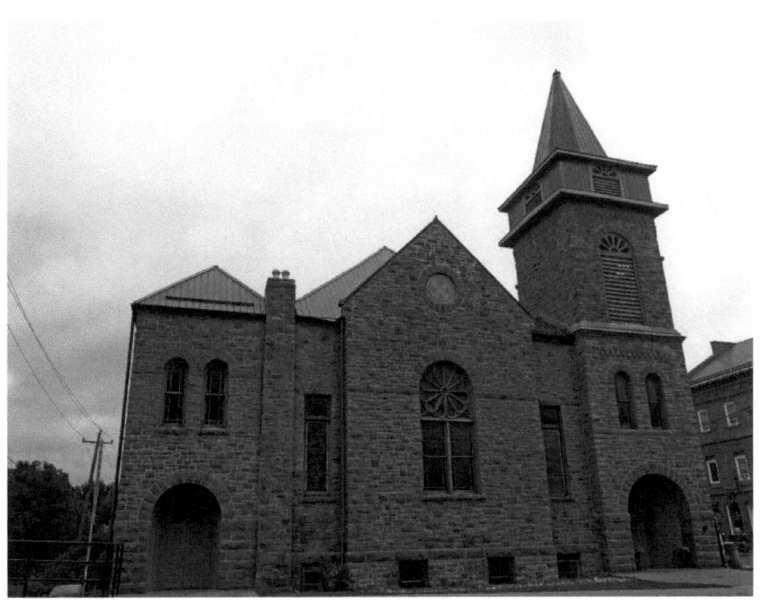

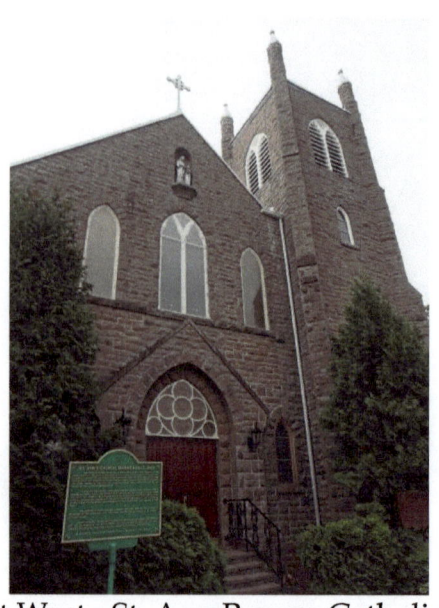

230 Main Street West - St. Ann Roman Catholic Church - 1903
Gothic – lancet windows, rose-type window

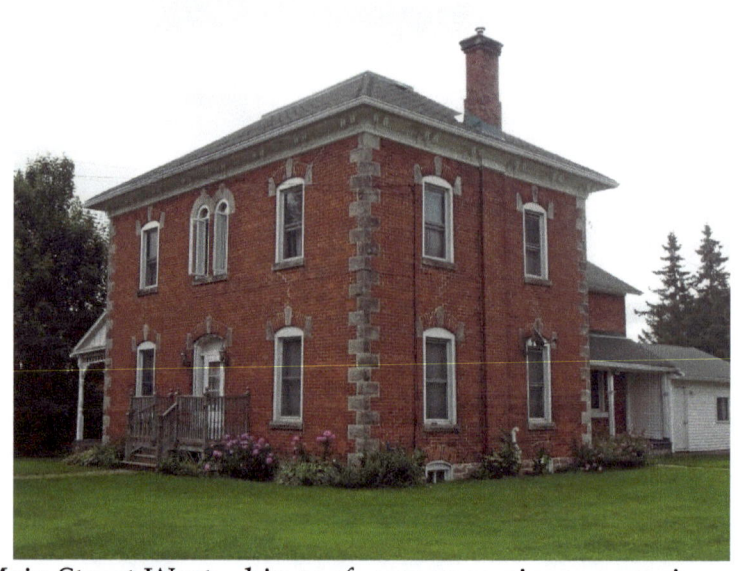

Main Street West – hip roof, corner quoins, voussoirs and
keystones

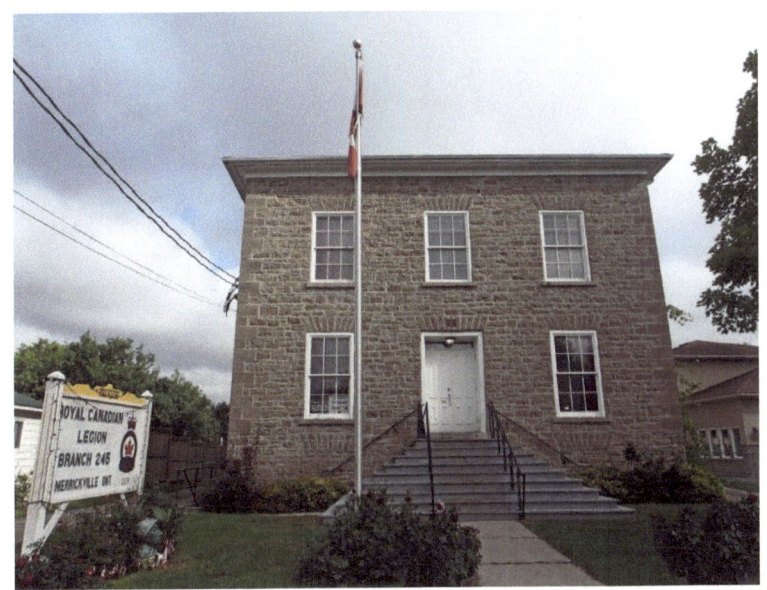

223 Main Street West - Royal Canadian Legion – old Town Hall - c. 1856 – stone, corner quoins

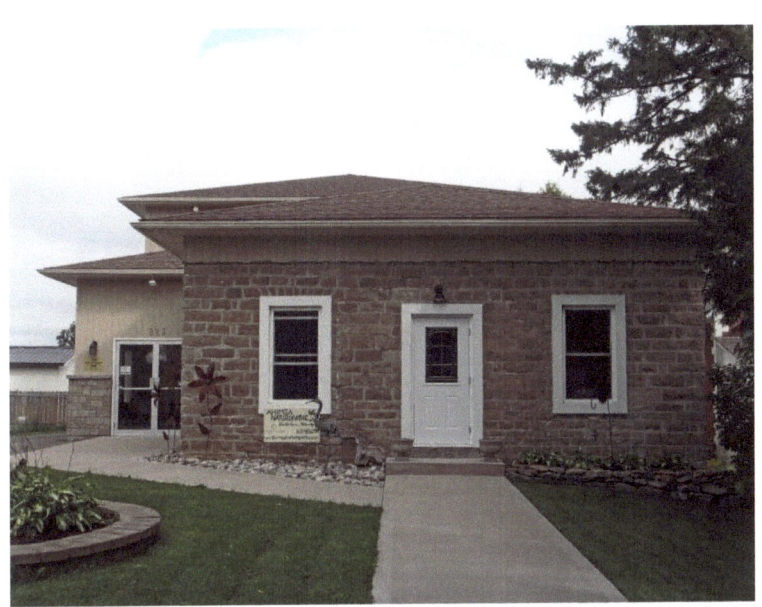

223 Main Street West – 1840 Guest House Bed & Breakfast – Regency Cottage

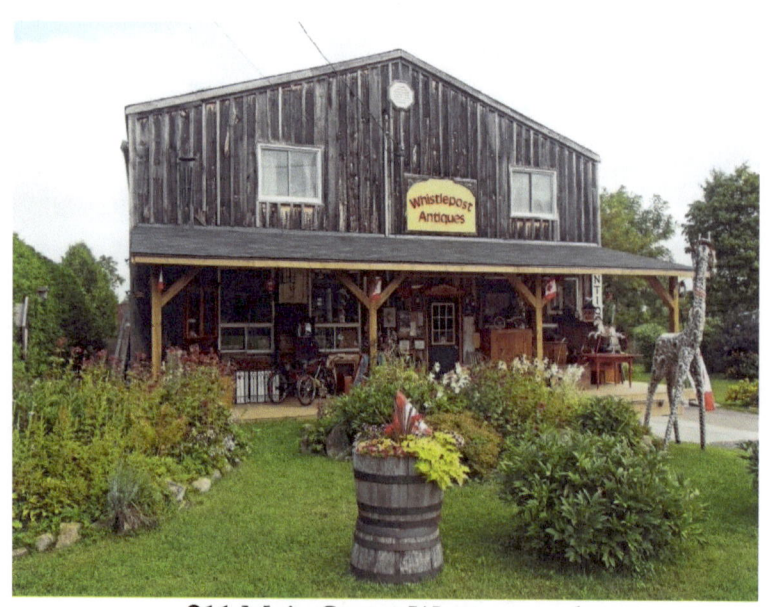

211 Main Street West - wood

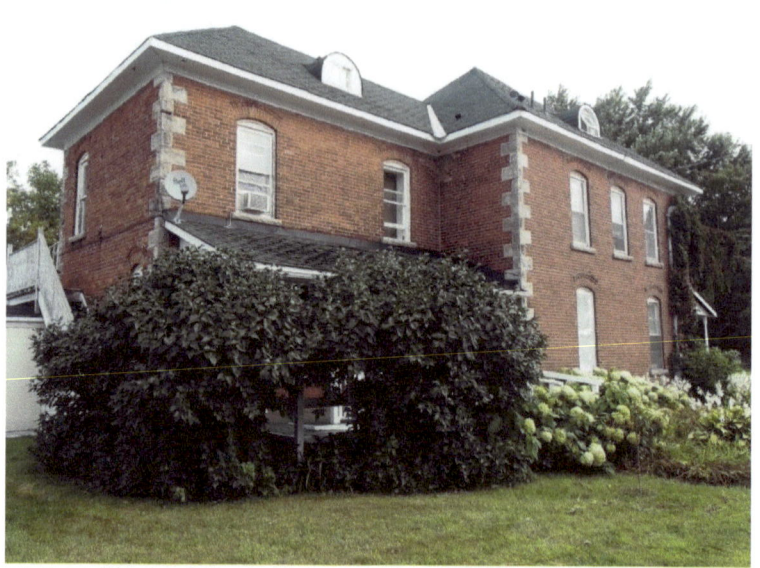

Main Street West – hip roof, dormers, corner quoins

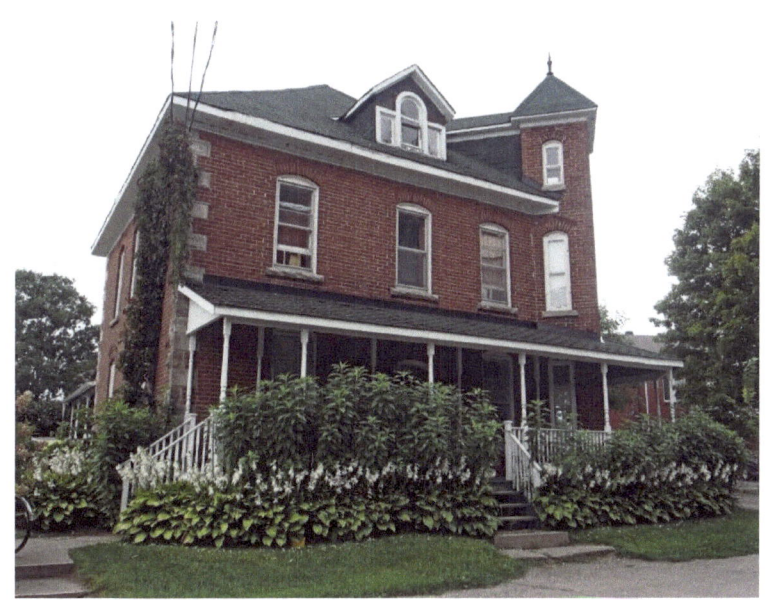

205 Main Street West – Queen Anne style – corner tower,
dormer with Palladian window, turned veranda roof
supports, open railing

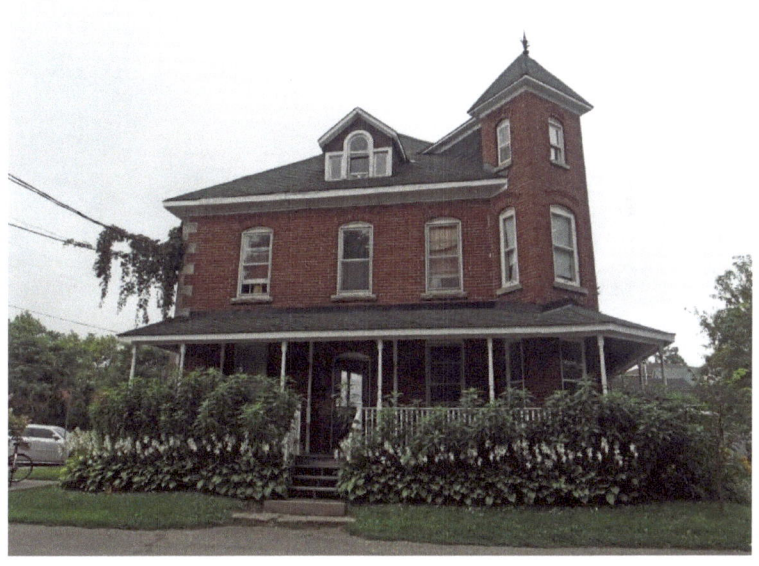

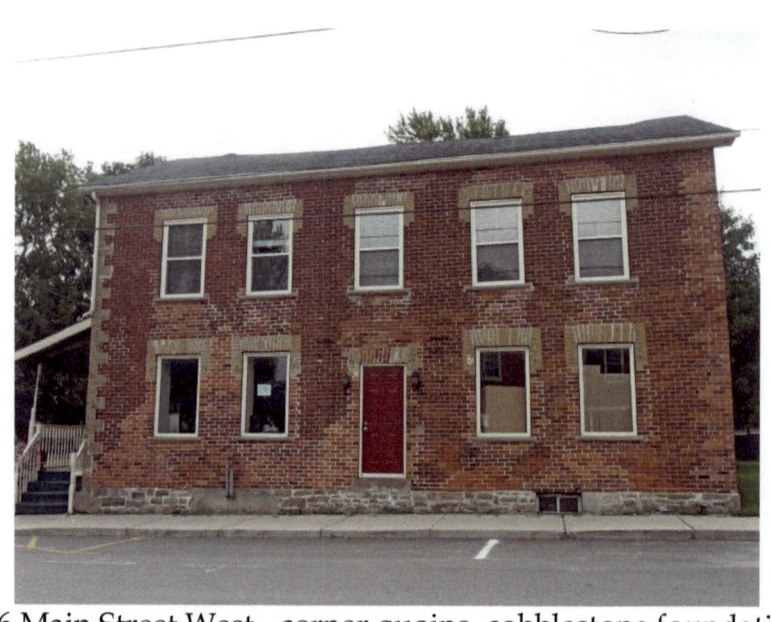

206 Main Street West - corner quoins, cobblestone foundation

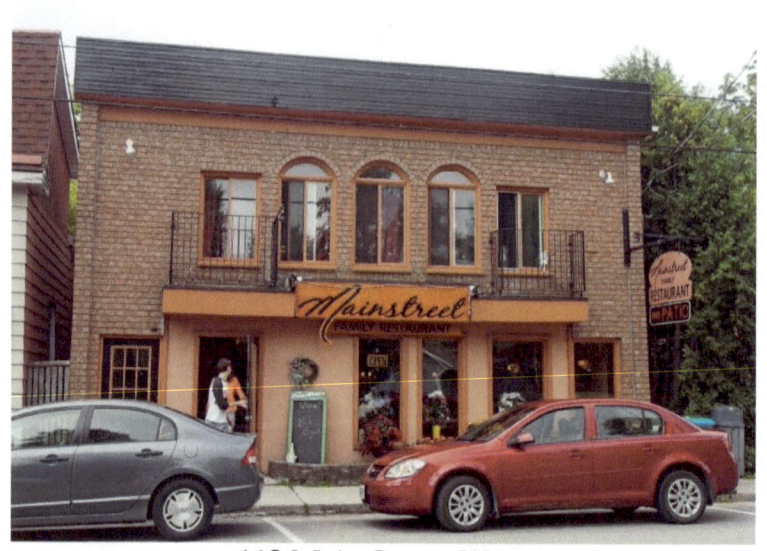

112 Main Street West

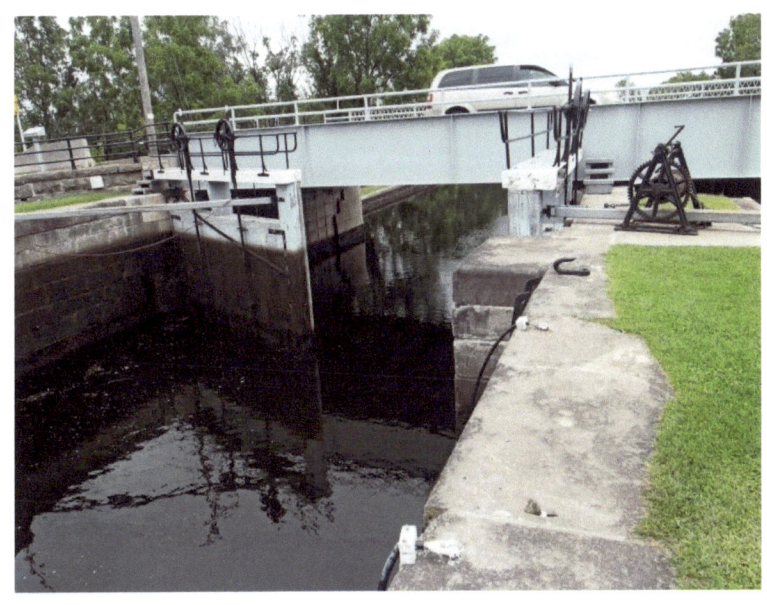

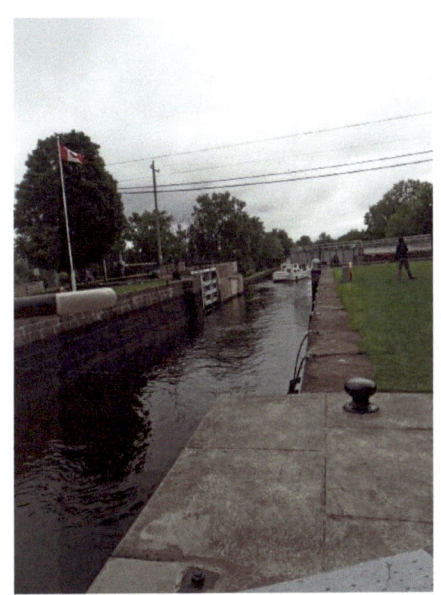
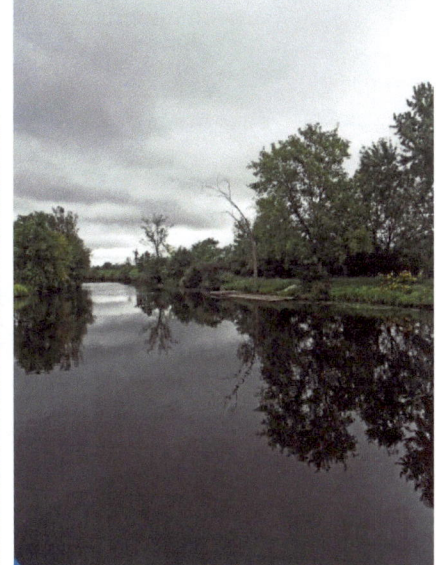

Lock

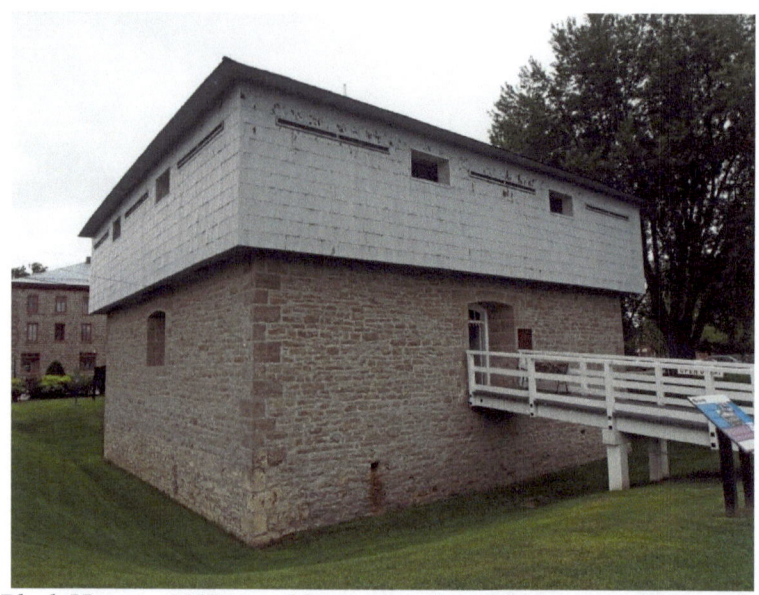

Block House – 1832 – could accommodate fifty men – 3.5 foot walls designed to withstand small cannon fire; pyramidal tin-sheathed roof to withstand torching; upper level overhang allowed for machicolated defense holes cut in the overhang to allow downward fire on an enemy; no military action here – served as lockmaster's quarters, a church, and a canal maintenance building – now a museum

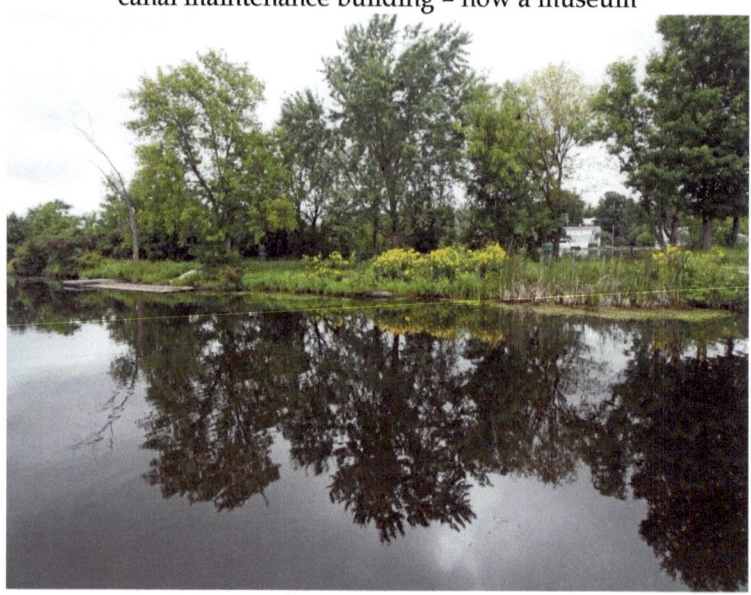

Rideau River

Stages in Land Settlement

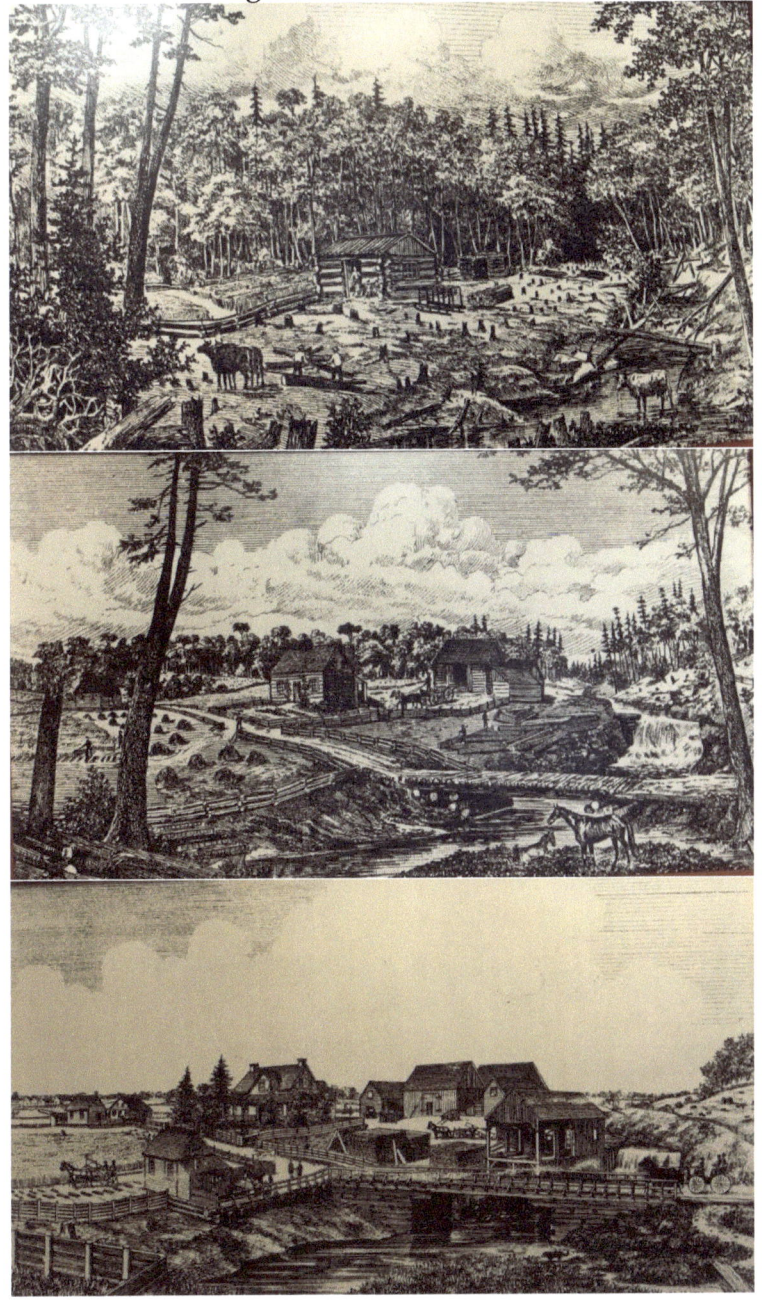

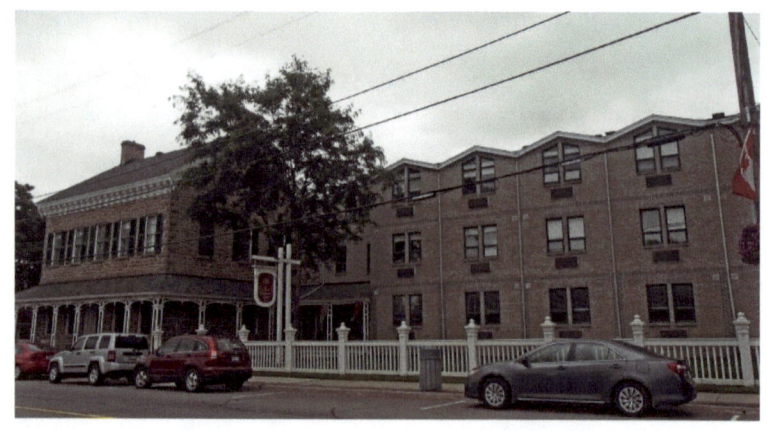

118 Main Street East – Sam Jakes House (prominent merchant) – c. 1861 – solid stone - now Fulford Preparatory College

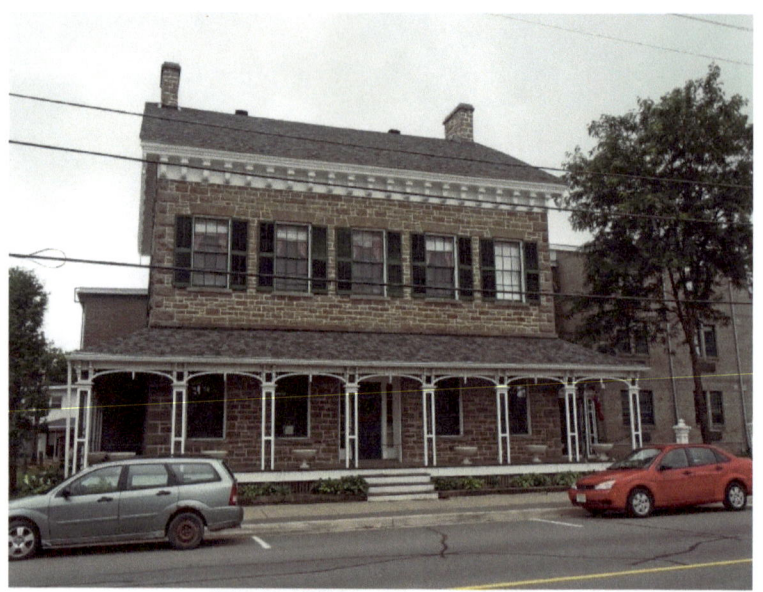

Cornice brackets, shutters

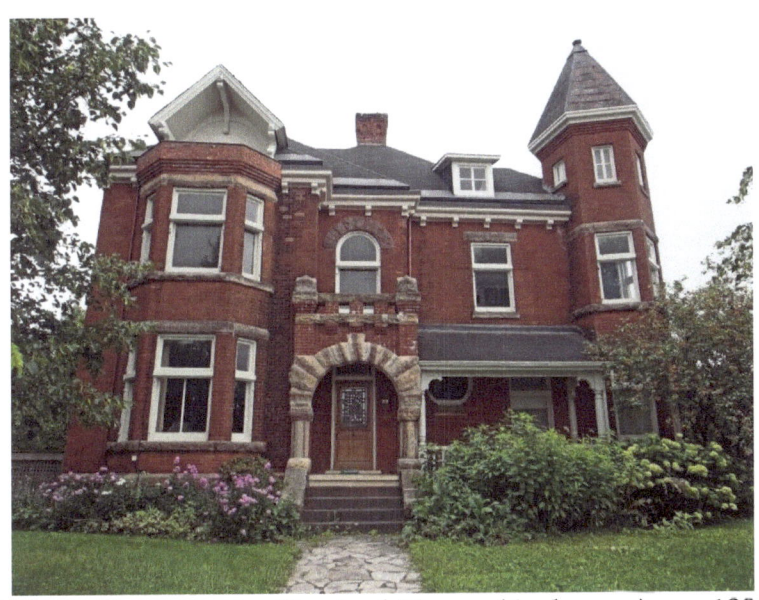

206 Main Street East – Percival House (Ardcaven) – c. 1890 – Richardsonian-Romanesque style – home of foundry-man Roger Percival – heavy stone arch around door, decorative chimney, two-storey bay window topped with open pediment, dormer, tower, stone courses

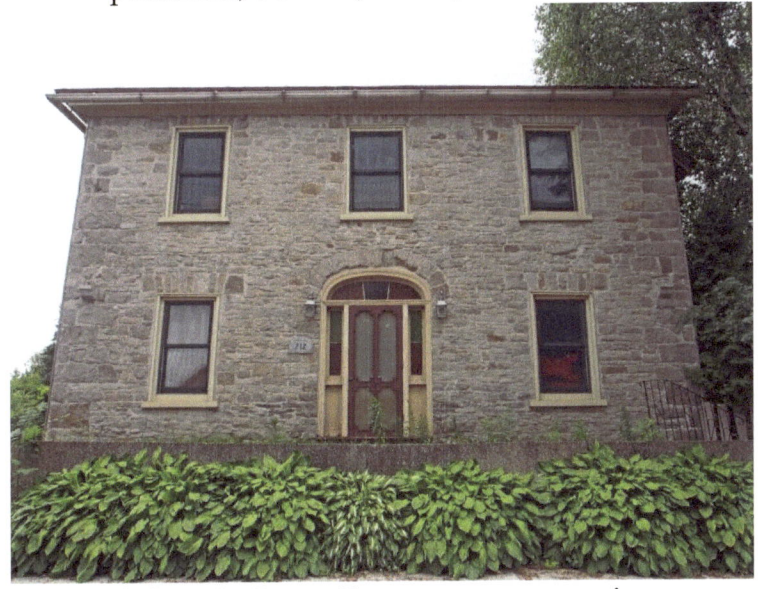

212 Main Street East – stone, voussoirs

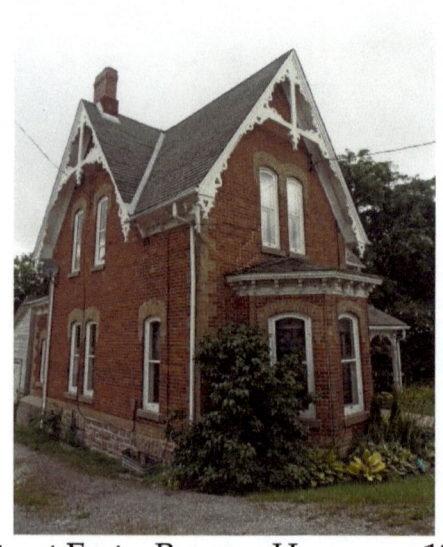

111 Main Street East – Pearson House – c. 1890 - Gothic Revival – former location of the Merrickville Public Library - verge board trim with finials on gables, dormer, bay window; veranda roof supports with ornate capital detailing

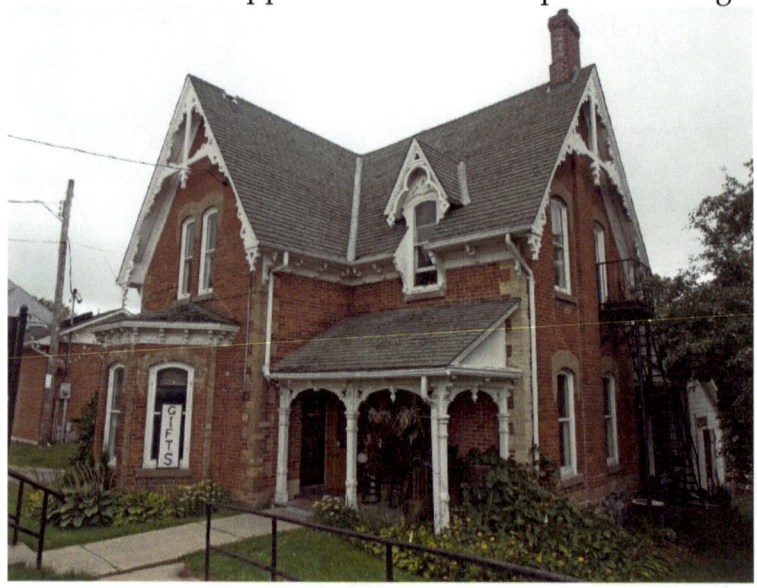

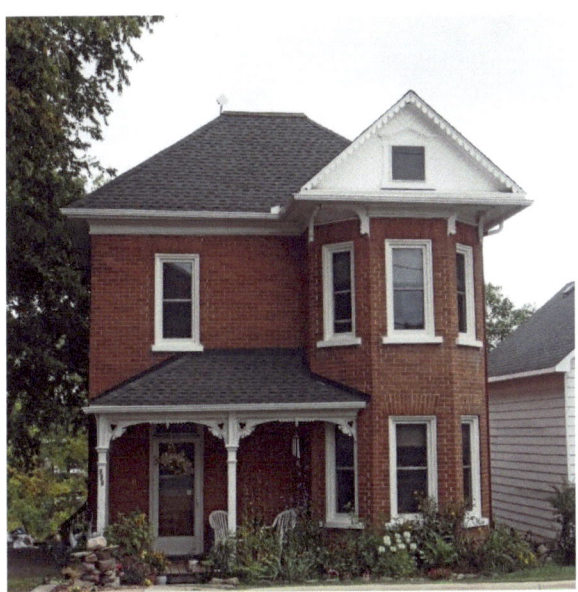

223 Main Street East – hip roof, two-storey bay window topped by pediment with fretwork supports; veranda roof supports with ornate capital detailing

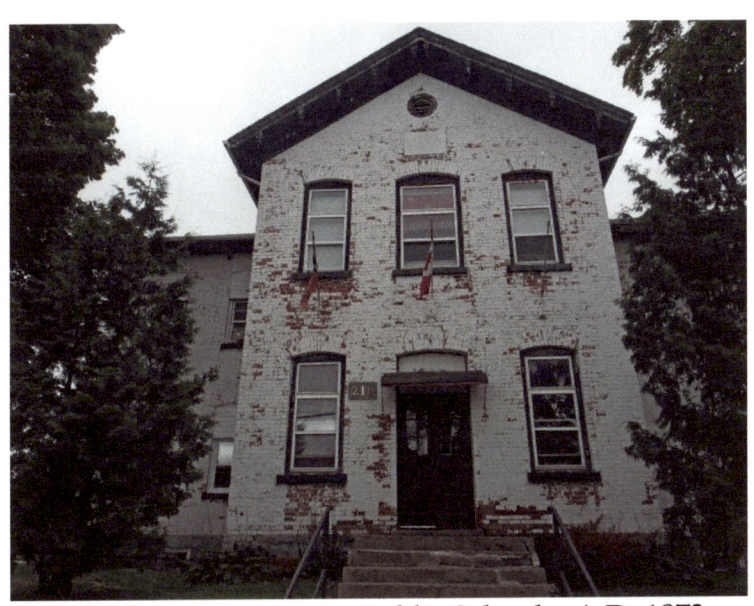

218 Main Street East – Public School – A.D. 1873

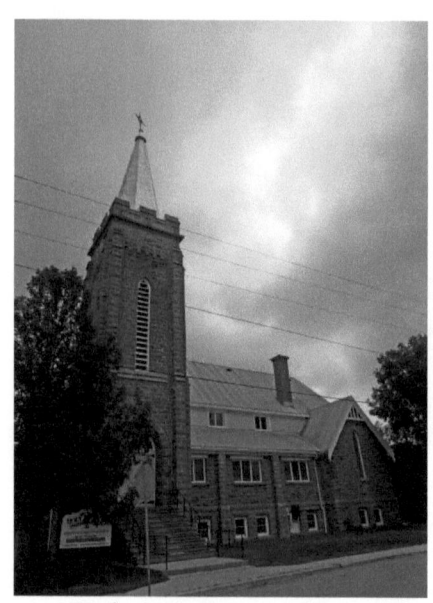

105 Church Street - Holy Trinity Anglican Church – A.D. 1908
– Gothic Revival – lancet windows, buttresses

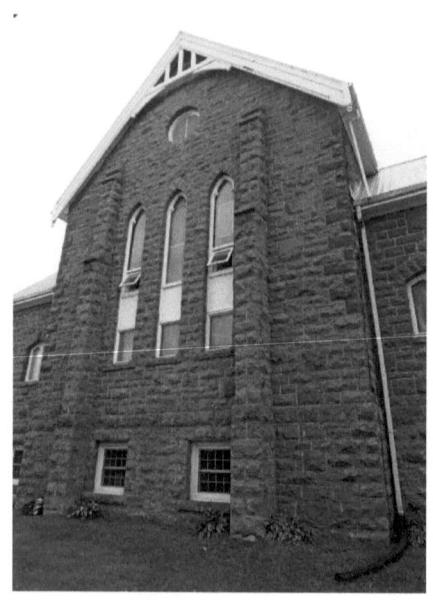

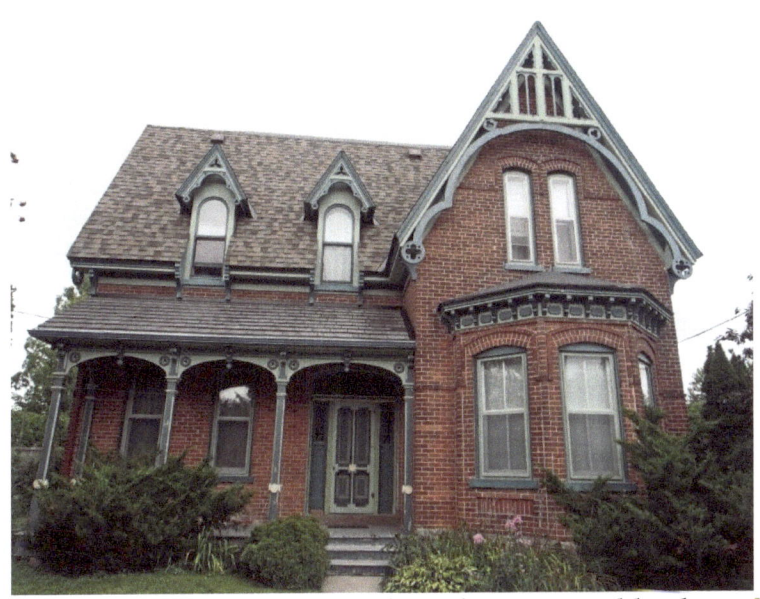

Church Street – Gothic – verge board trim on gable above bay
window, dormers, pillars with decorative capitals

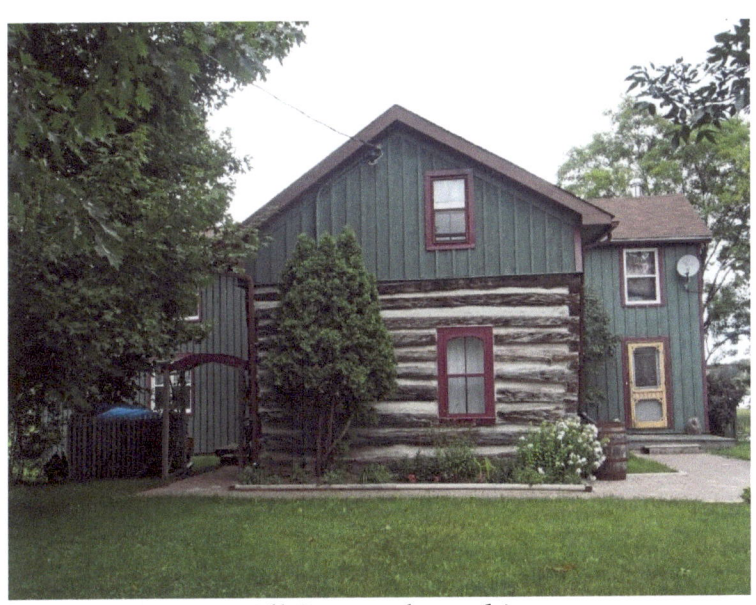

Mill Street – log cabin

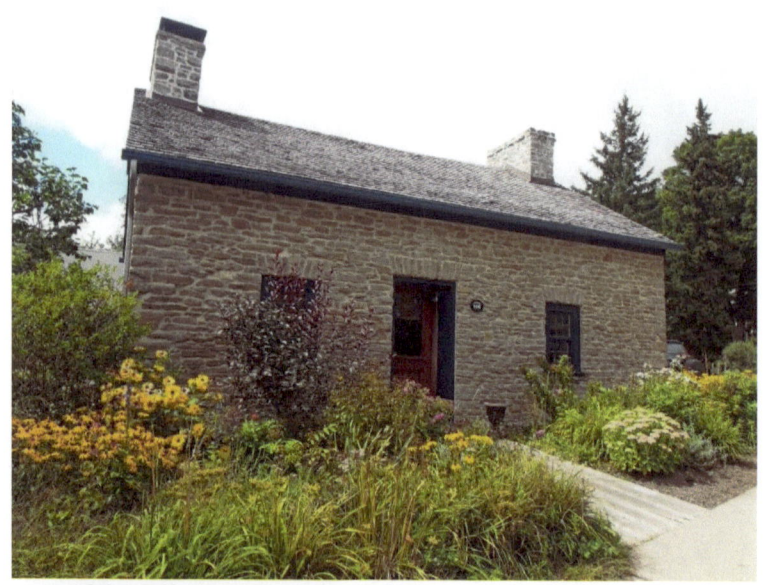

106 Mill Street – Merrick Tavern – 1832 - stone

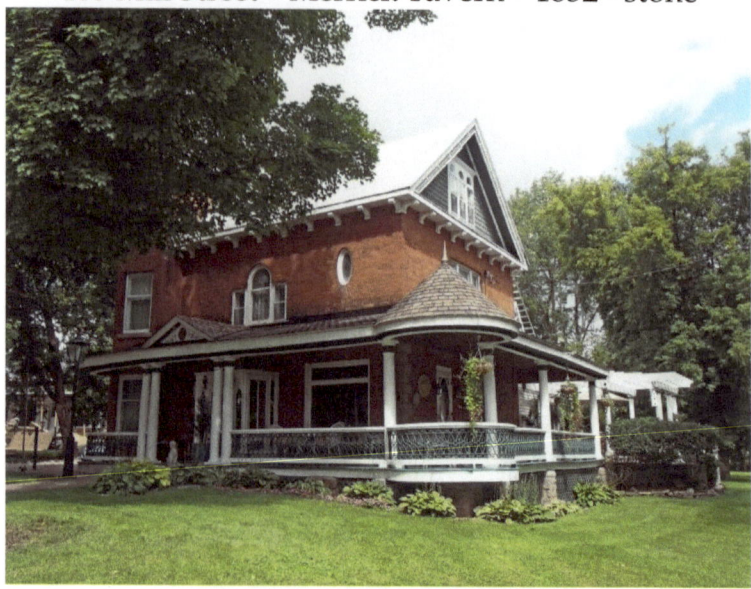

205 Mill Street – The Magee House – c. 1845 – Queen Anne style – wraparound veranda, Doric veranda supports, open railing, Palladian window, oval window, cornice brackets – now operated as the Millisle Bed and Breakfast

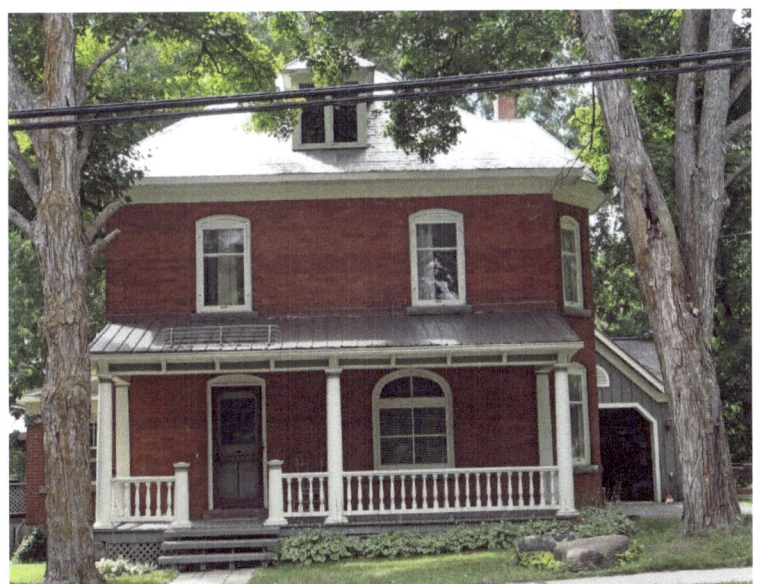

206 Mill Street – hip roof, dormer, open railing

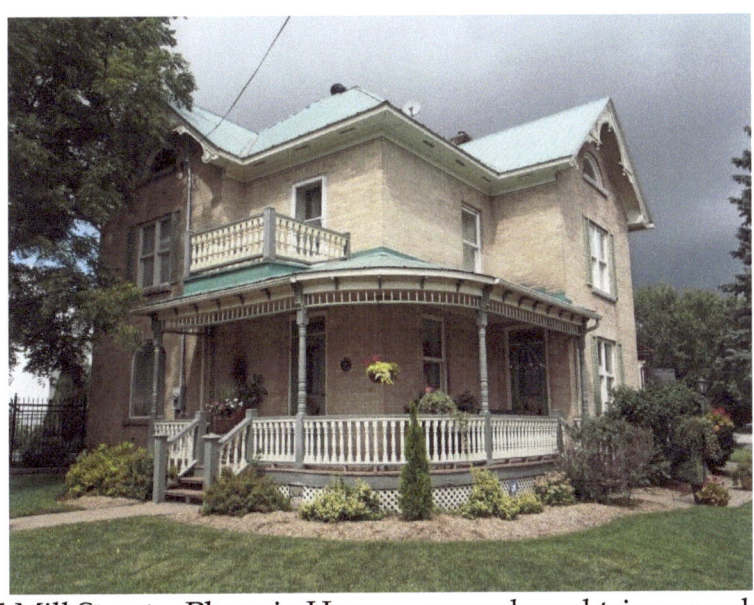

305 Mill Street – Phoenix House – verge board trim on gables, second floor balcony, turned veranda roof supports with spindles under cornice, open railing

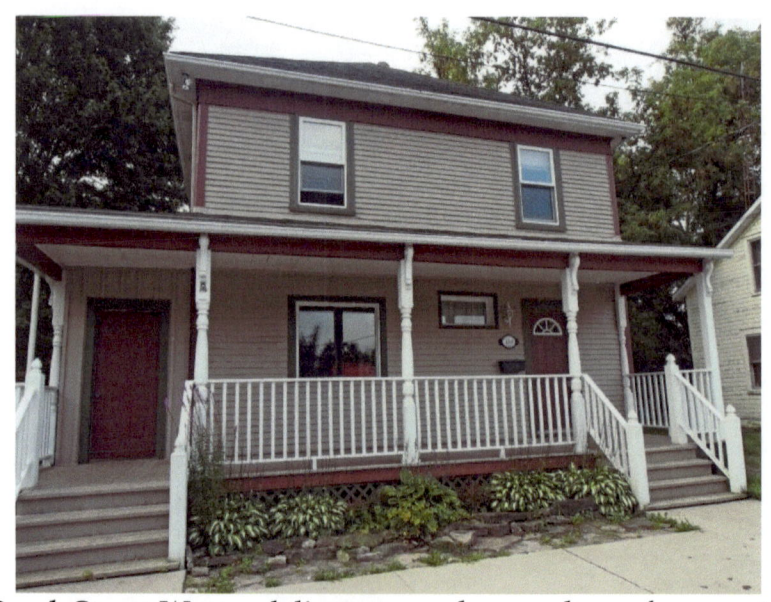

Brock Street West – delicate turned veranda roof supports, open railing

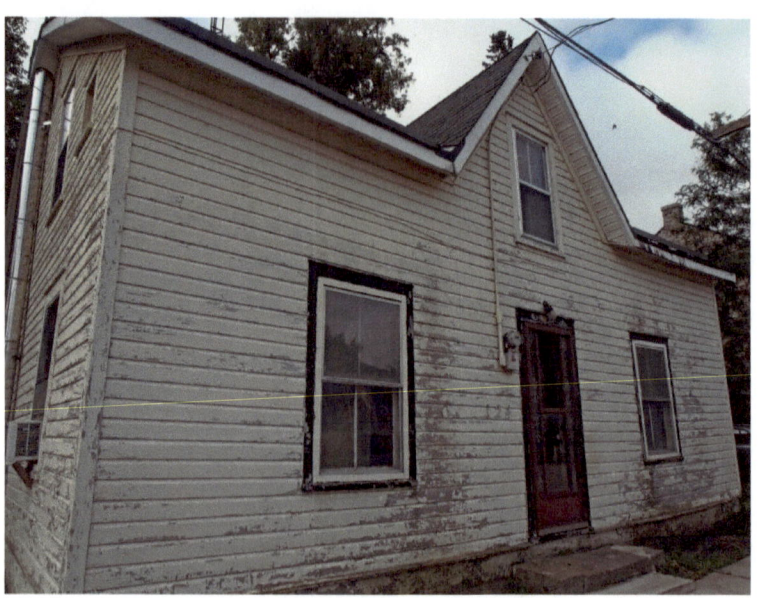

Brock Street West - Gothic

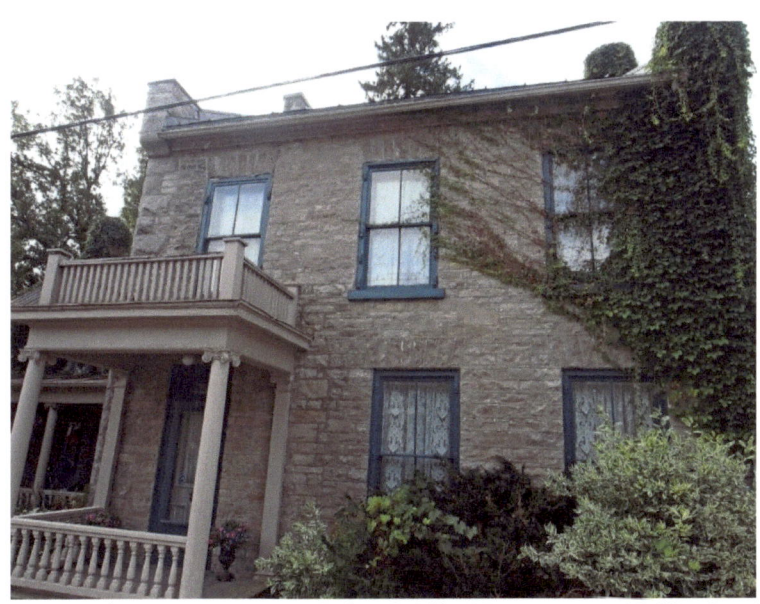

130 Brock Street West – John Mills House – c. 1860 - Ionic capitals on porch supports with second floor balcony above; parapeted end gables to help prevent spread of roof fires to neighbours

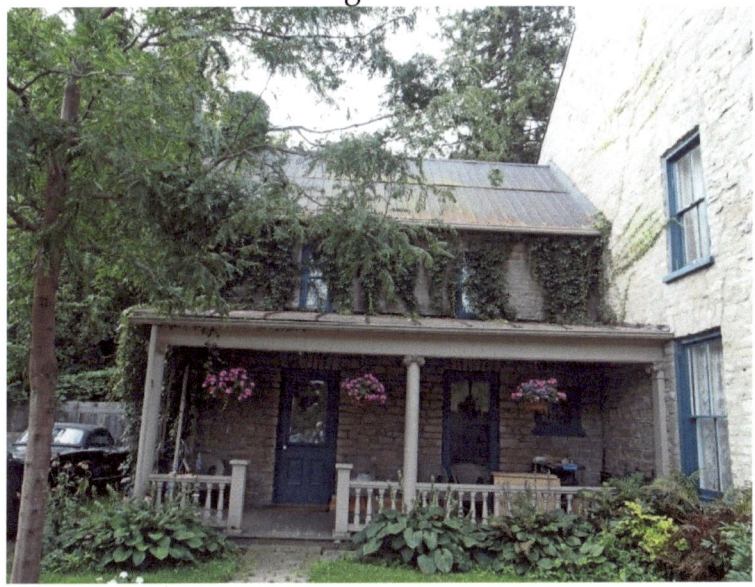

Constructed as a store and furniture factory by cabinet maker John Mills

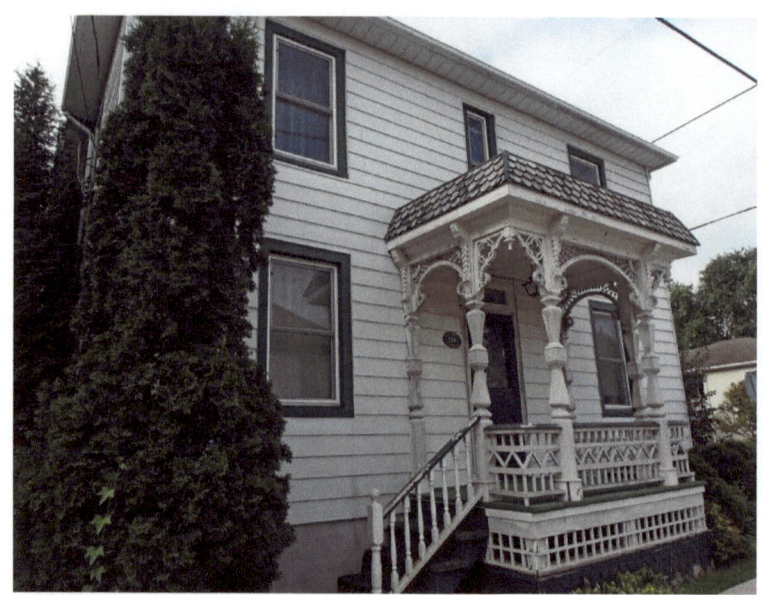

136 Brock Street West – decorative support posts and ornate capital details to make a very impressive entrance

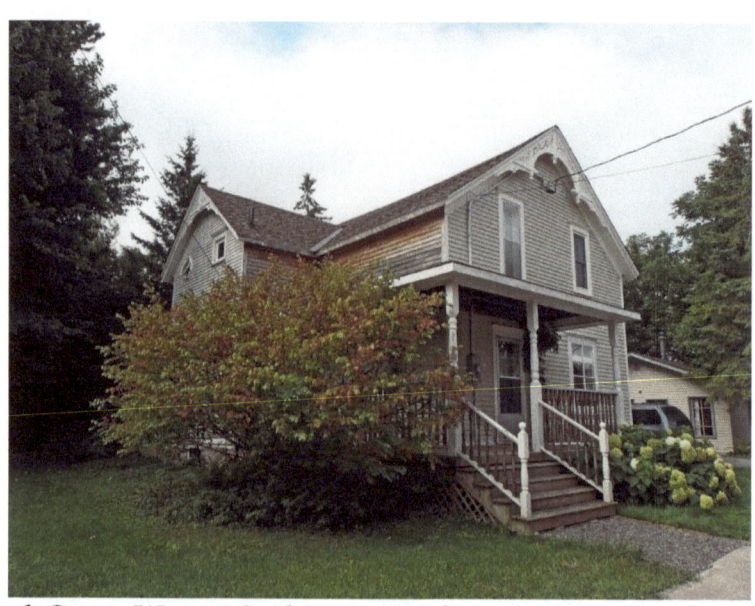

Brock Street West – Gothic – verge board trim on gables with finials

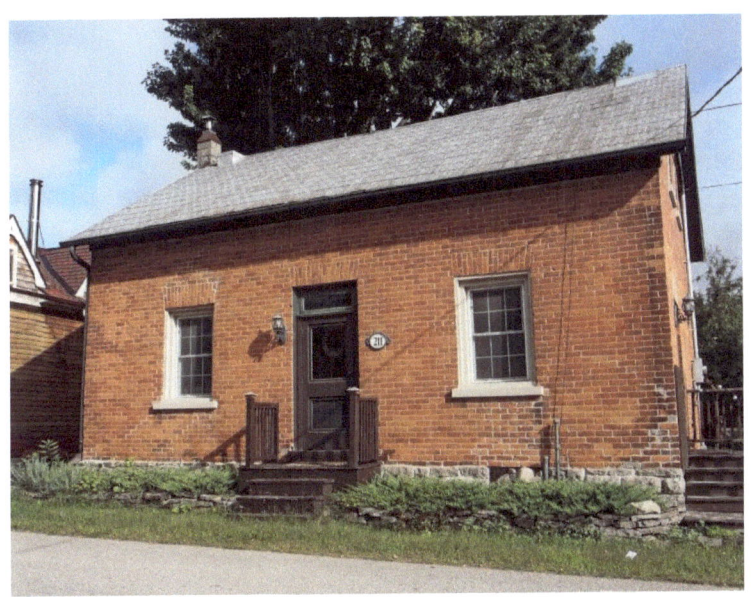

211 Brock Street West

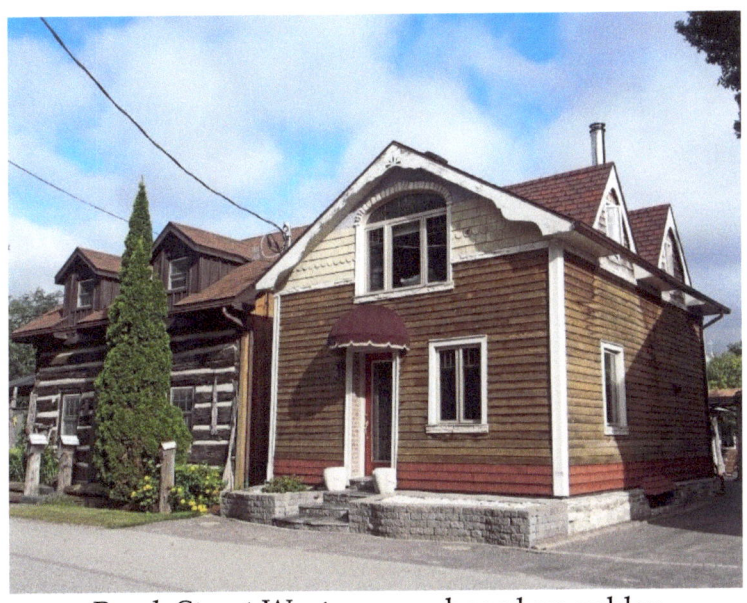

Brock Street West – verge board on gables

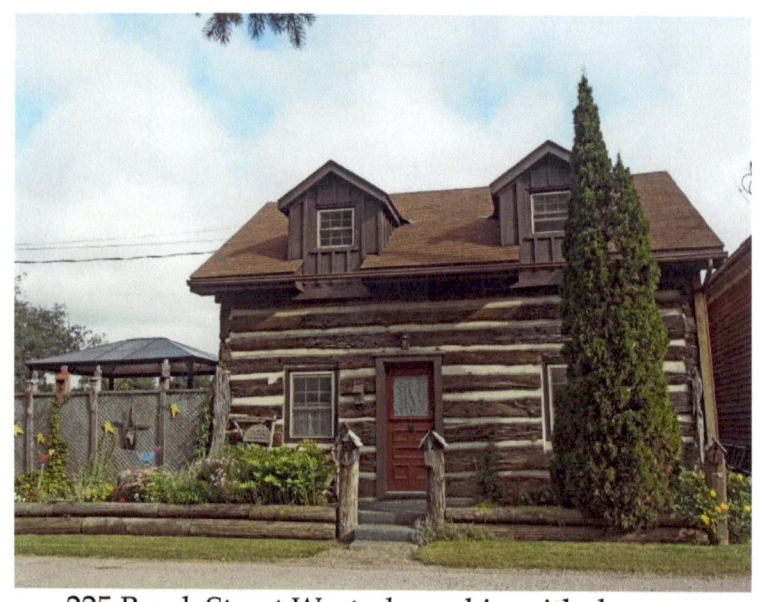

225 Brock Street West - log cabin with dormers

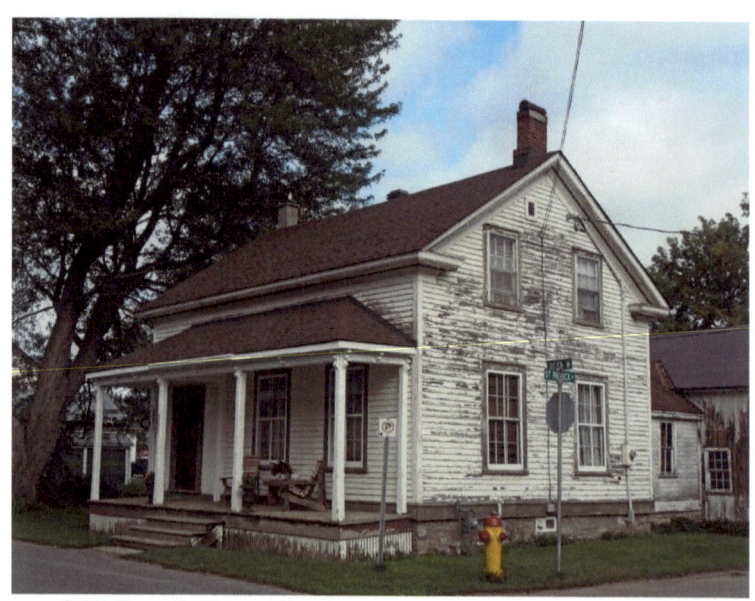

305 Brock Street West – cornice return on gable

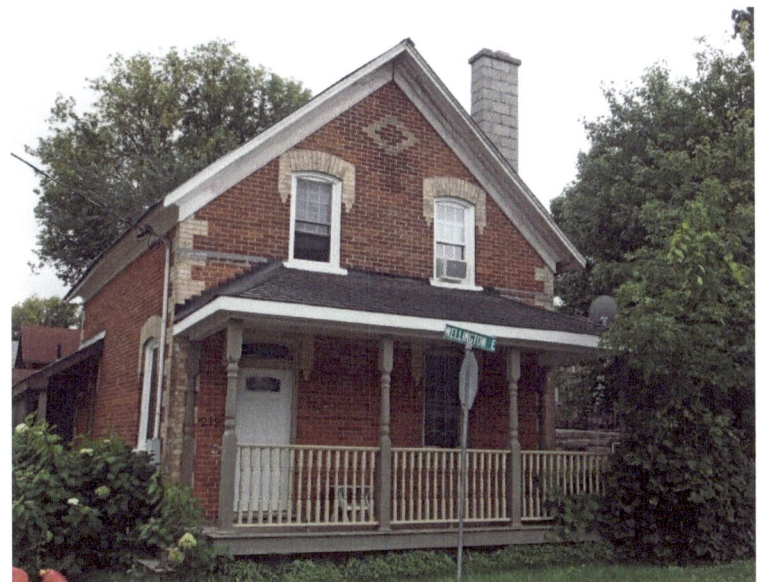

218 Wellington Street East – Gothic – dichromatic brickwork on quoins and voussoirs; turned veranda roof supports, open railing

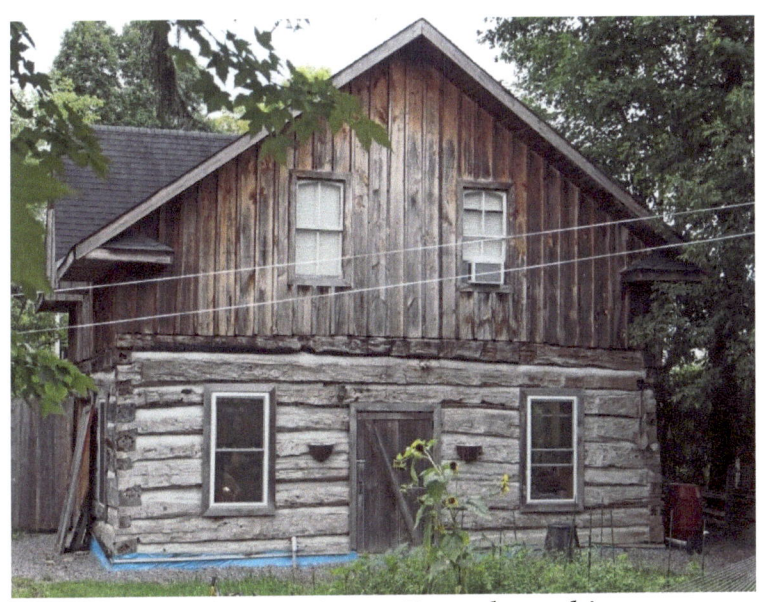

Wellington Street East – log cabin

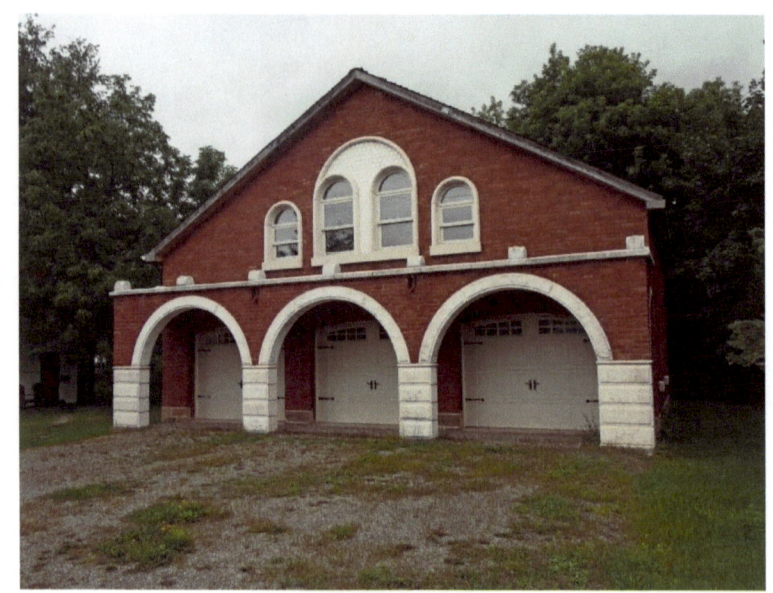

Elgin Street

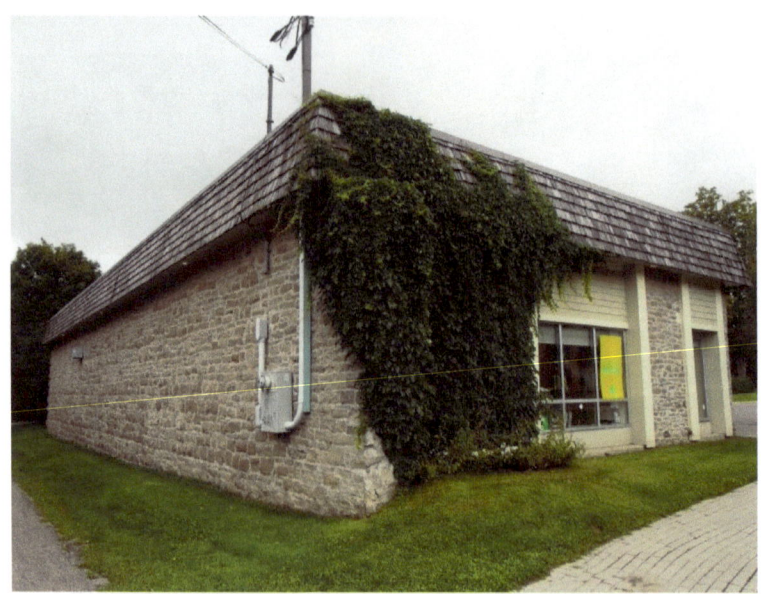

Elgin Street – Liquor Store – 1860 foundry of H. D. Smith

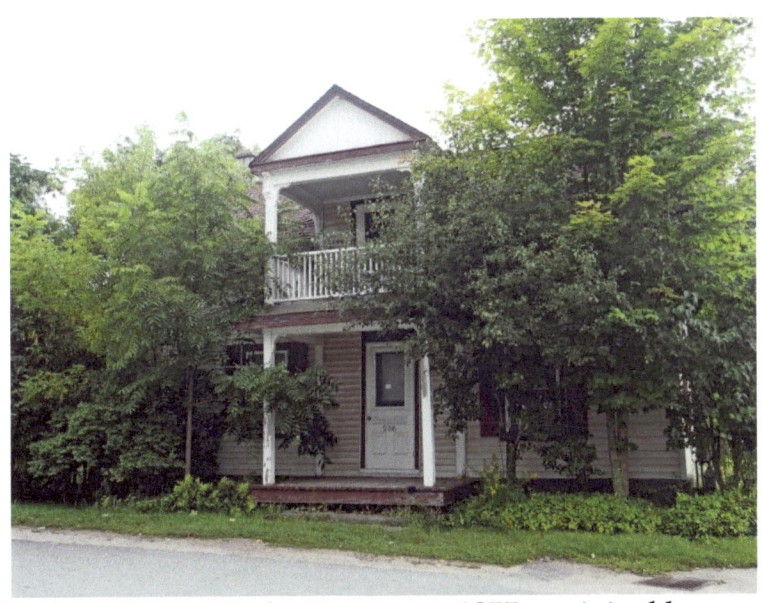

206 Elgin Street – Duke House – c. 1855 – original logs now covered with wooden shipboard siding

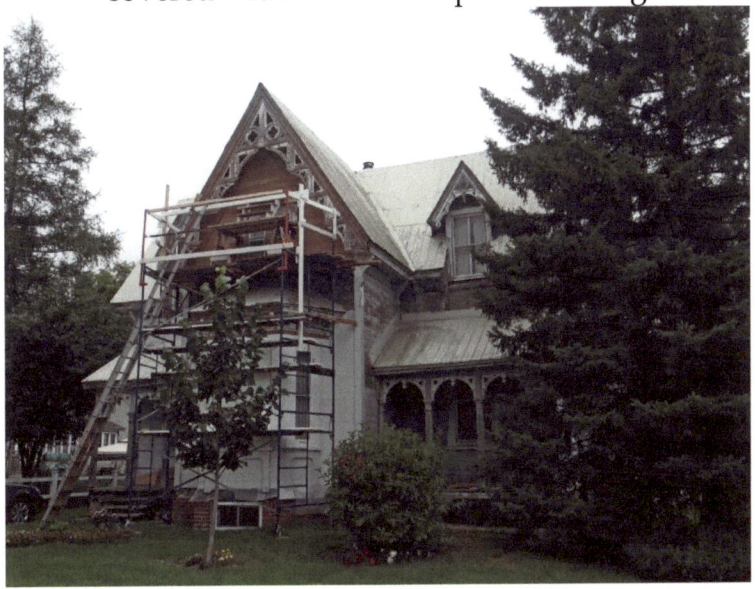

306 Elgin Street – elegant wooden gabled home built by Merrickville master builder Samuel Langford as a wedding gift for his daughter – Gothic – verge board trim on gable and dormer, decorative capitals on veranda supports

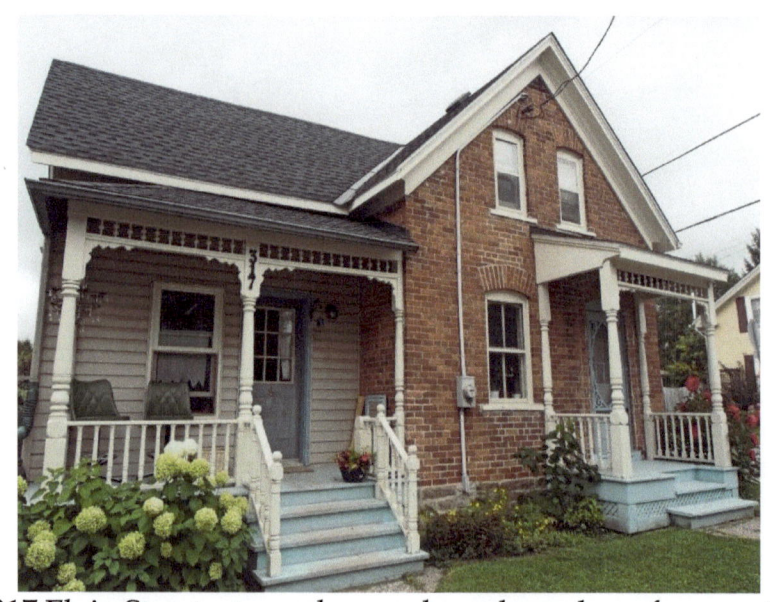

317 Elgin Street – turned veranda and porch roof supports with spindles under cornice

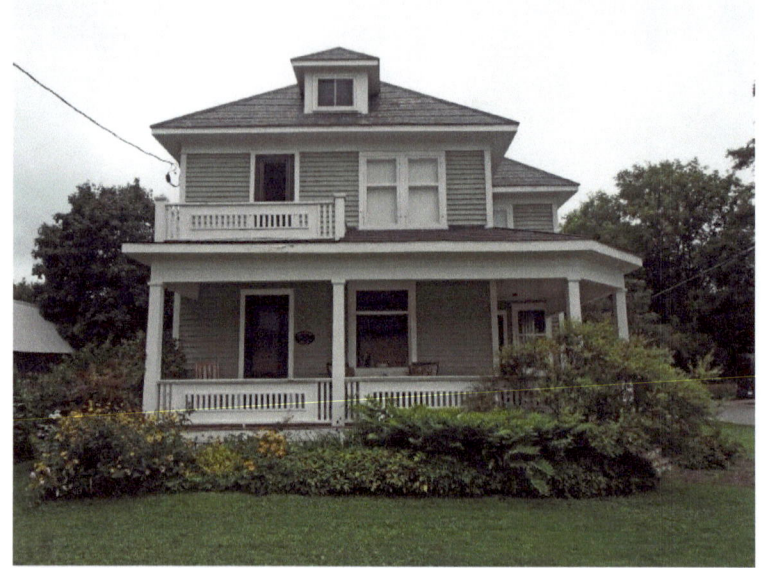

406 Elgin Street – Morrison House – hip roof, dormer, second floor balcony with open railing to match that of first floor wraparound verandah

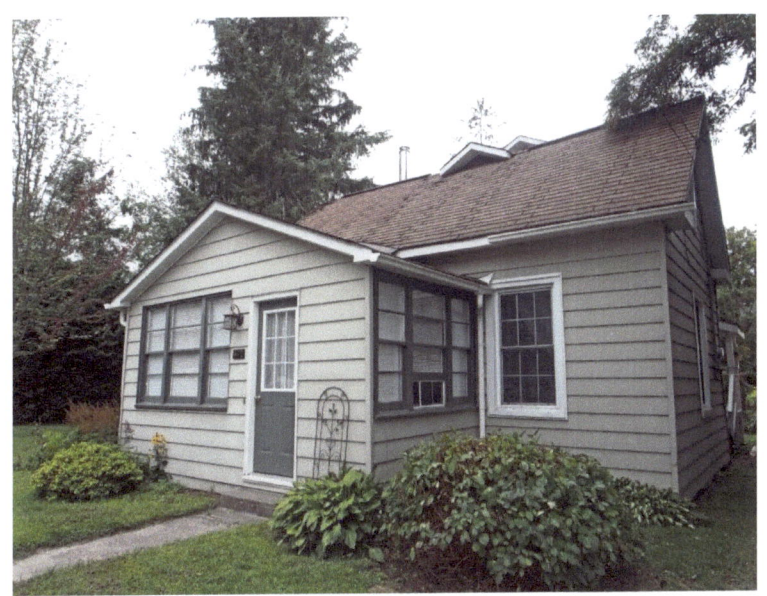

412 Elgin Street

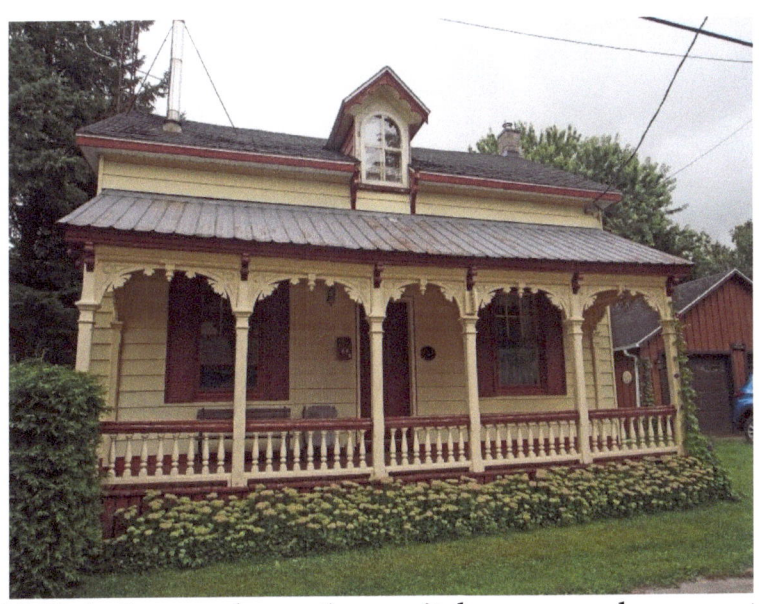

405 Elgin Street - decorative capitals on veranda supports,
open spindle railing; dormer in attic

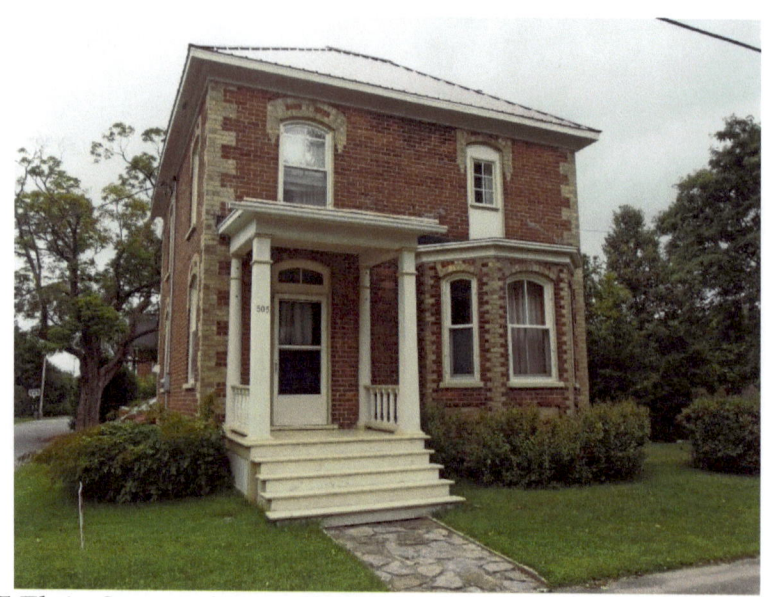

505 Elgin Street – hip roof, dichromatic voussoirs and quoins, bay window

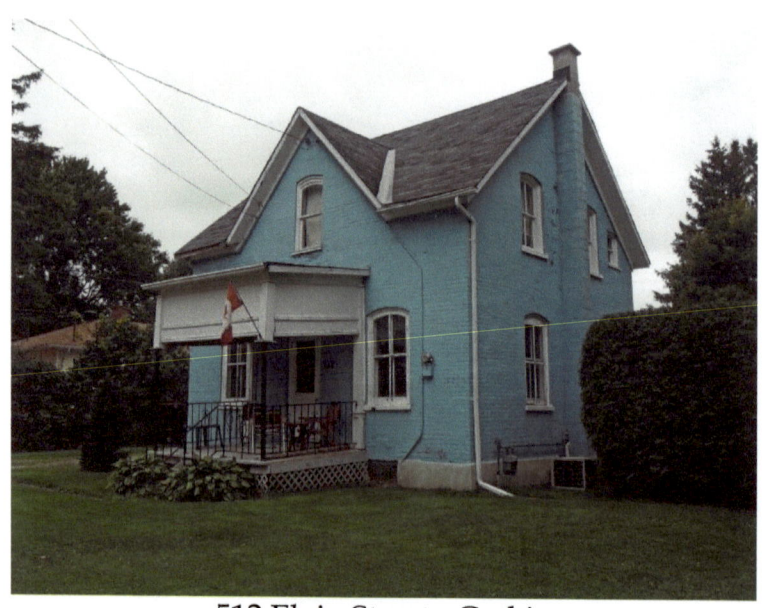

512 Elgin Street - Gothic

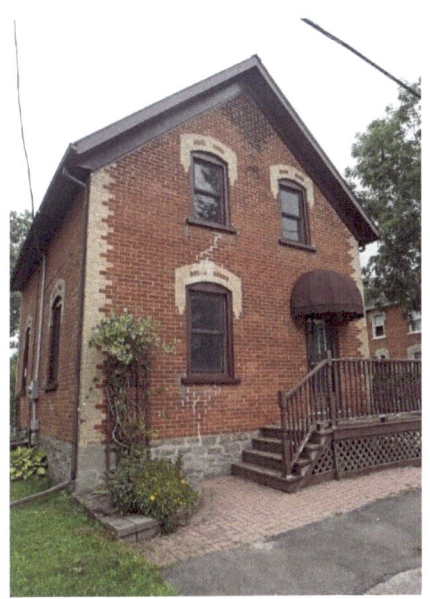 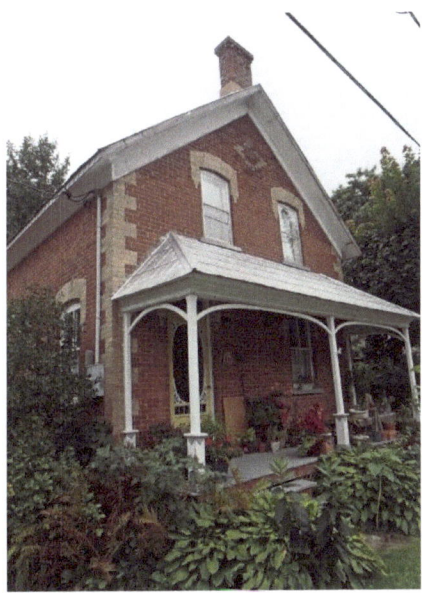

511 Elgin Street   605 Elgin Street

Gothic – dichromatic voussoirs and quoins

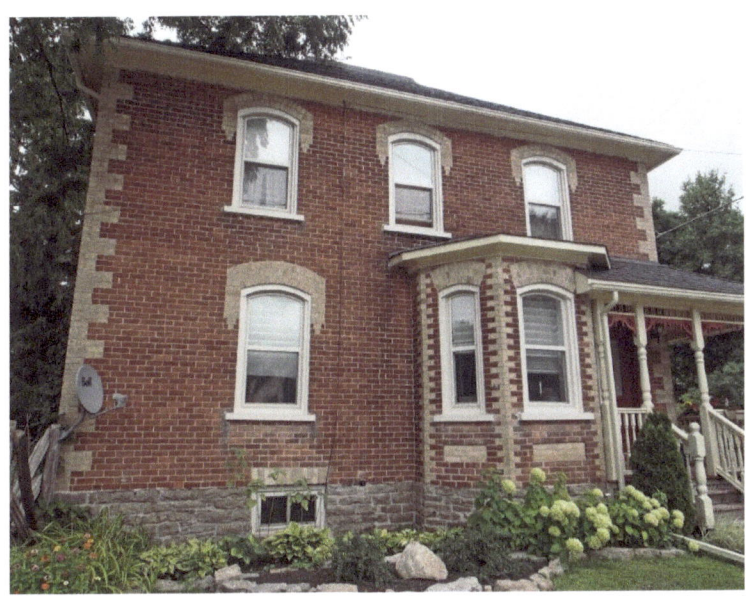

Elgin Street - hip roof, dichromatic voussoirs and quoins, bay window, turned porch supports with decorative capitals

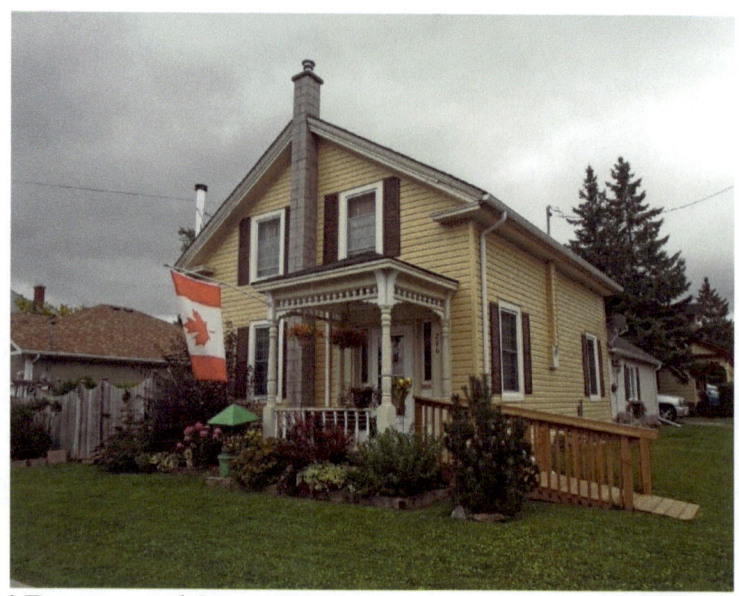

206 Drummond Street East – cornice return on gable, porch supports with decorative capitals

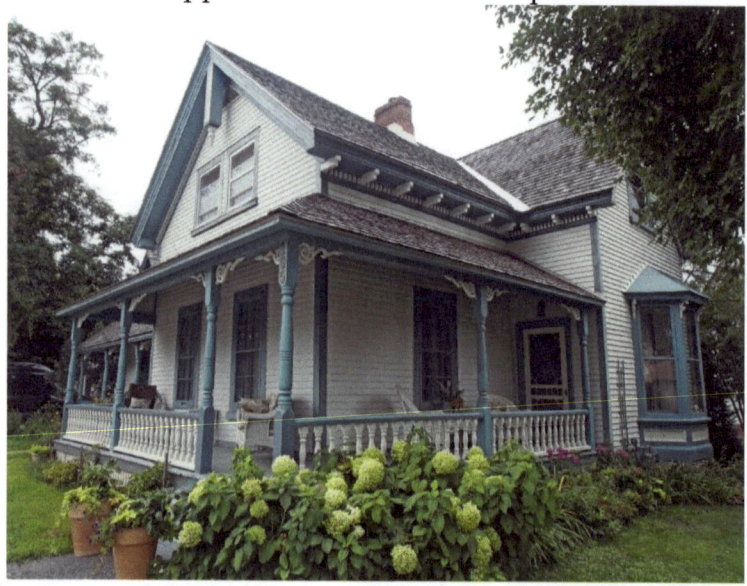

Drummond Street East – Gothic – finial on gable, cornice brackets and dentil molding, turned supports with decorative capitals on wraparound veranda, open railing, bay window

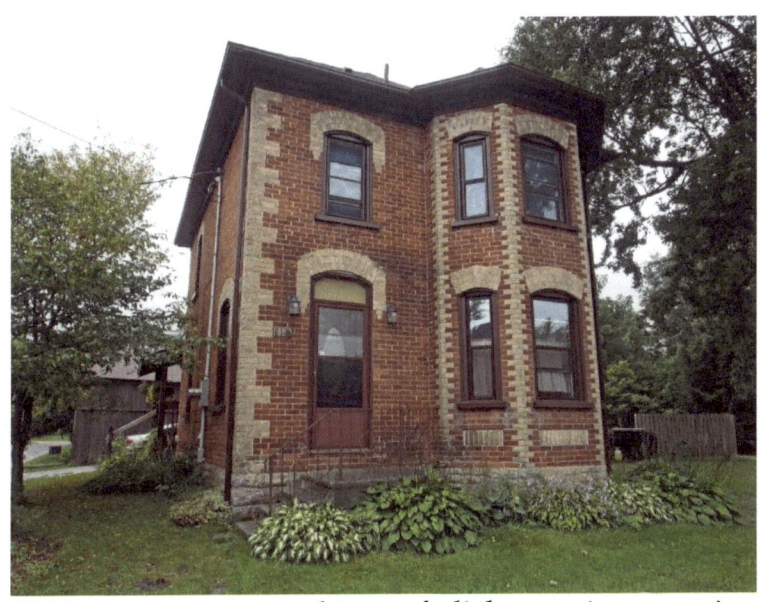

118 Colborne Street East - hip roof, dichromatic voussoirs and quoins, two-storey bay window

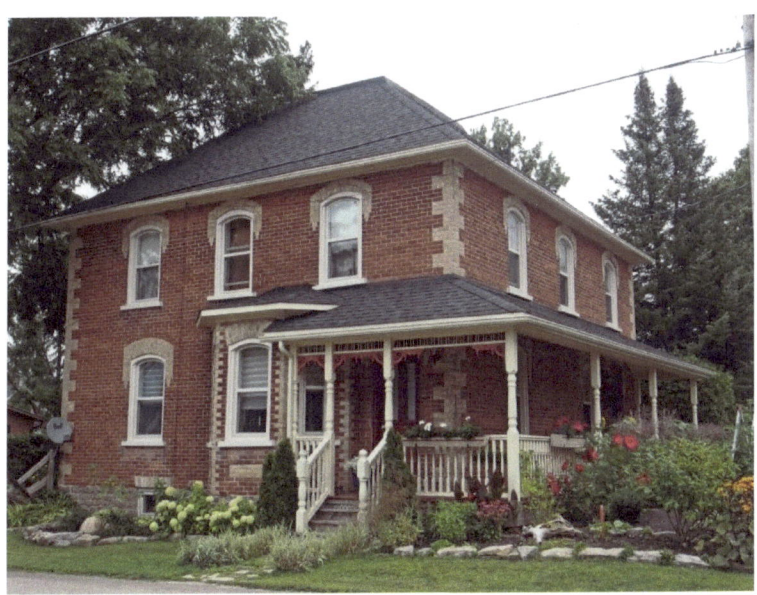

Colborne Street East - - hip roof, dichromatic voussoirs and quoins, bay window, turned supports with decorative capitals on wraparound veranda, open railing

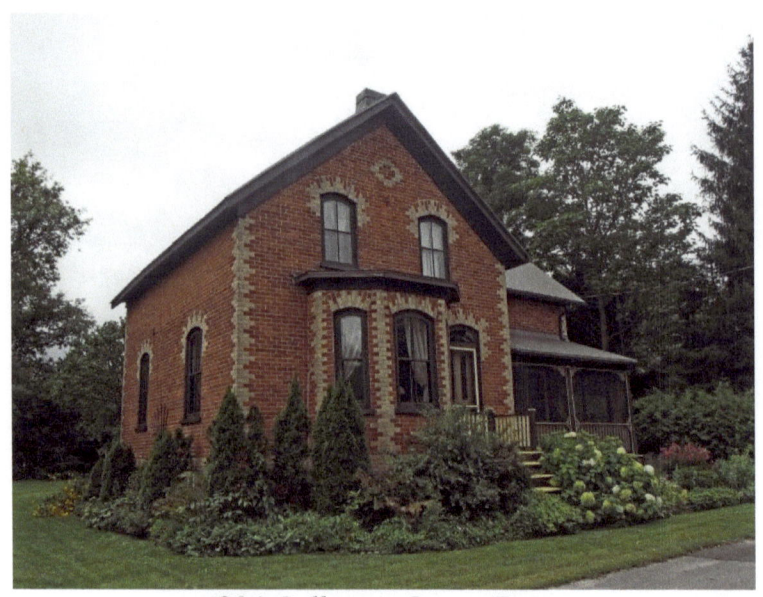

206 Colborne Street East

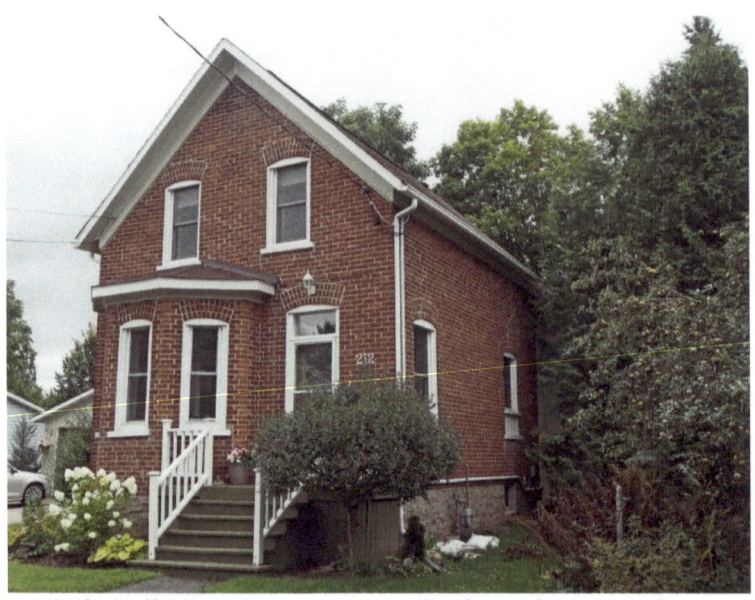

212 Colborne Street East – Gothic – bay window

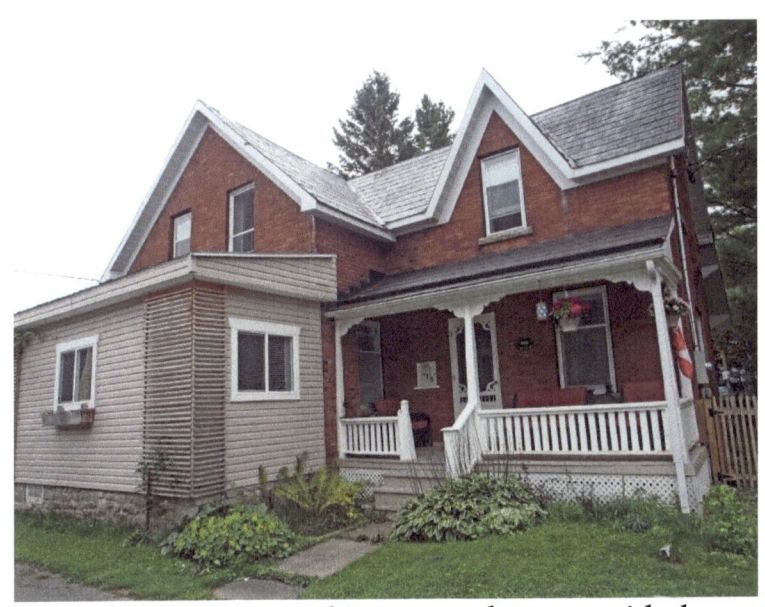

218 Lewis Street East – Gothic – veranda posts with decorative capitals

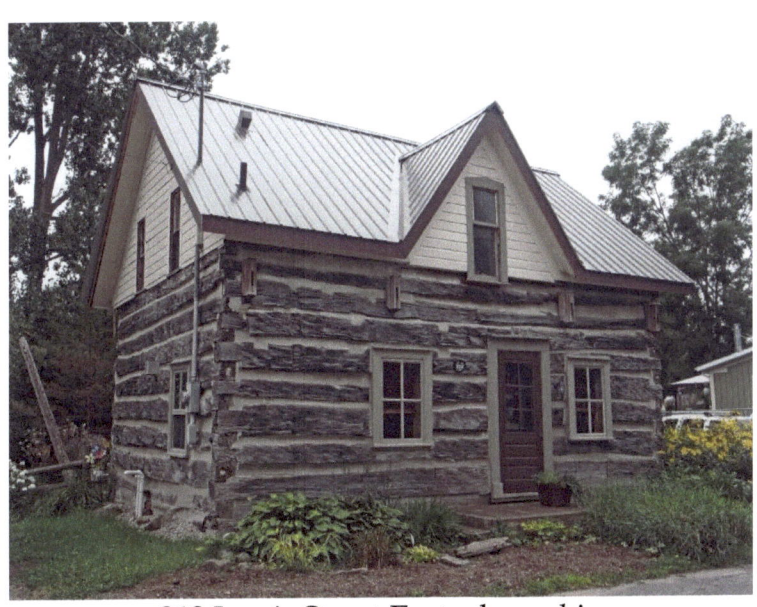

212 Lewis Street East – log cabin

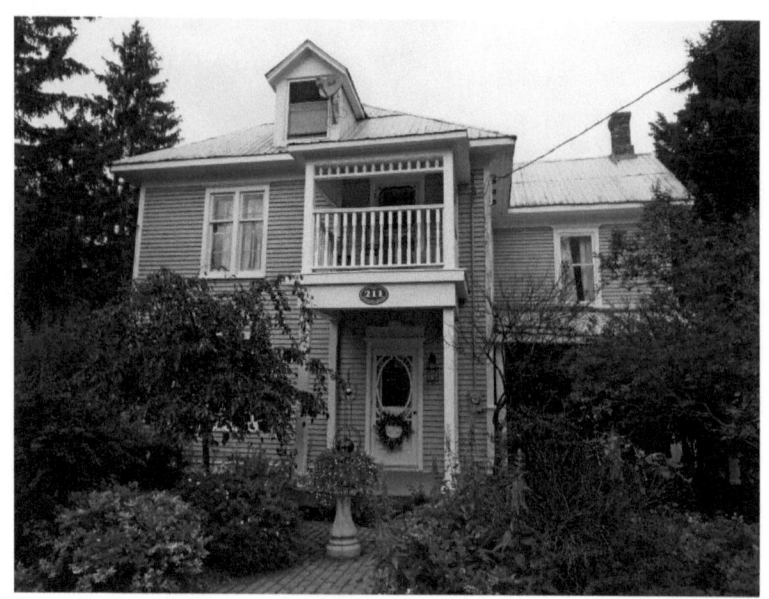

211 Lewis Street East – hip roof, dormer, second floor balcony

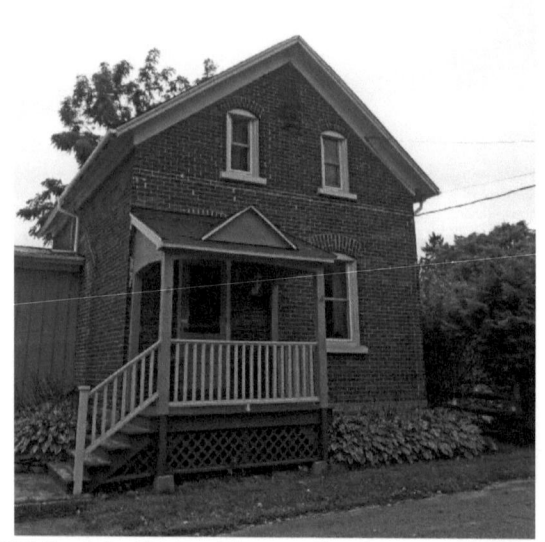

206 Lewis Street East – Gothic - pediment

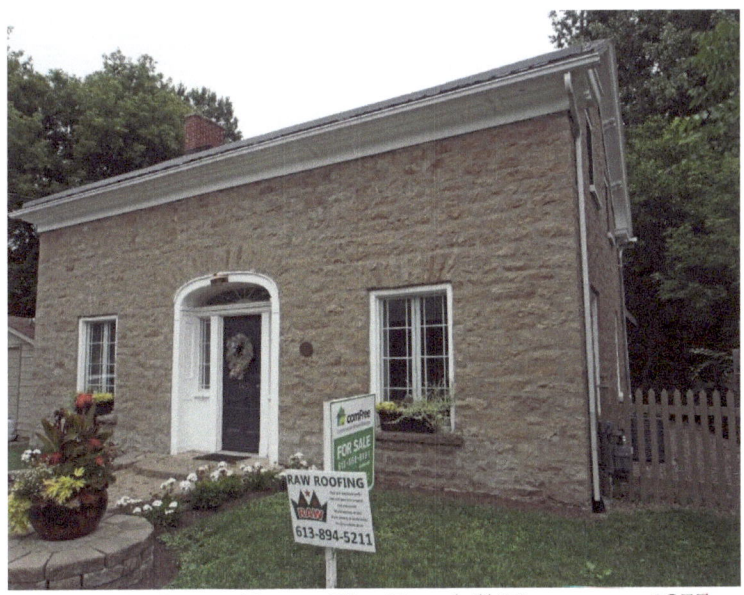

105 Lewis Street East – The Tyndall House – c. 1855 – Adamesque style stone house with an earlier style Loyalist doorway and trim details

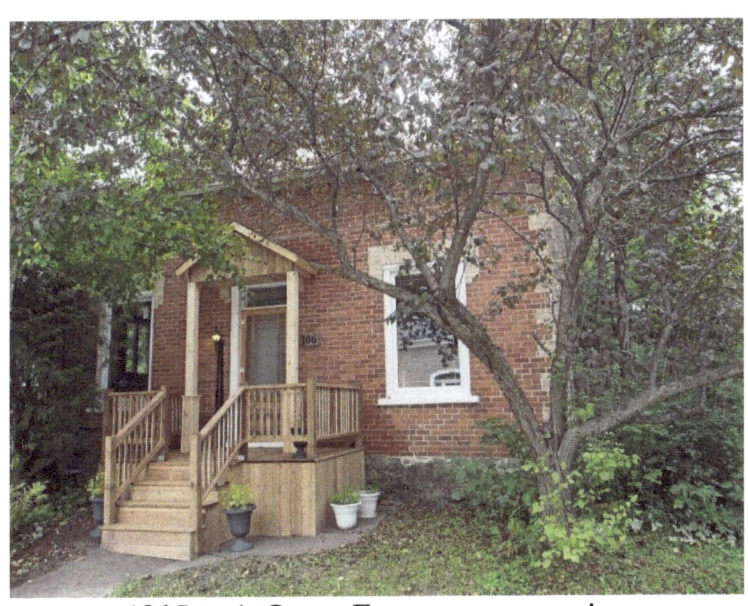

106 Lewis Street East – corner quoins

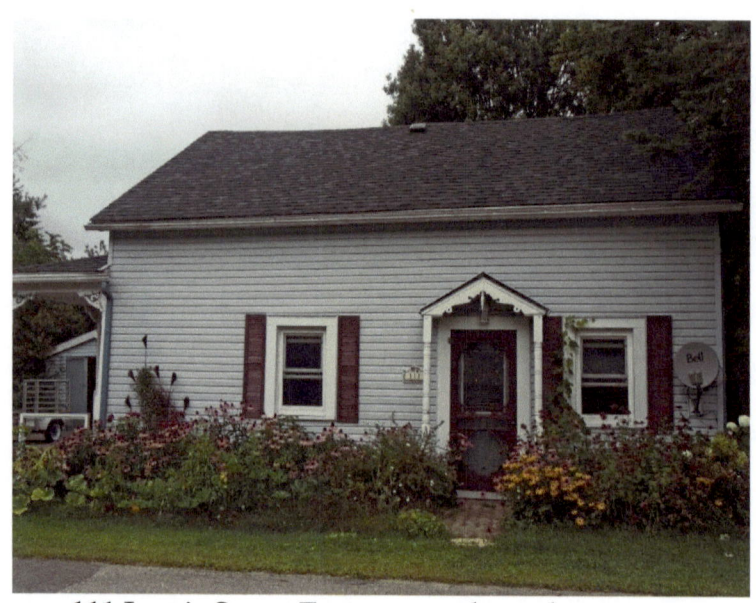

111 Lewis Street East – turned porch supports

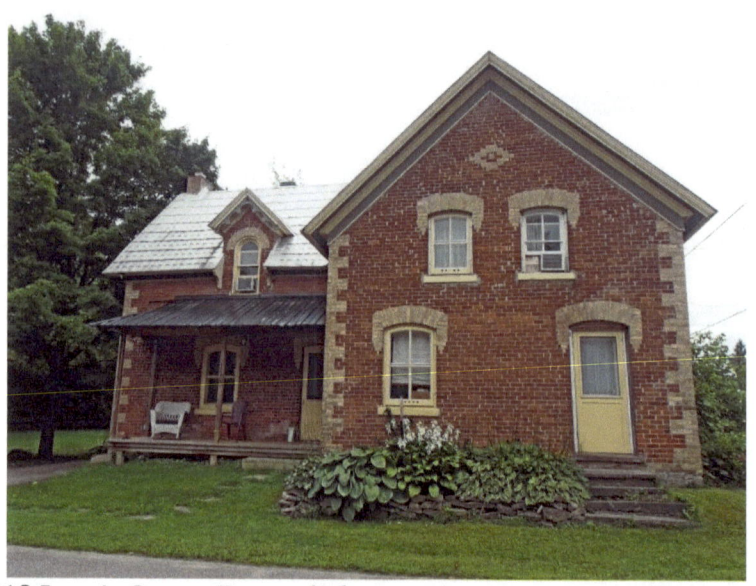

118 Lewis Street East - dichromatic voussoirs and quoins, dormer

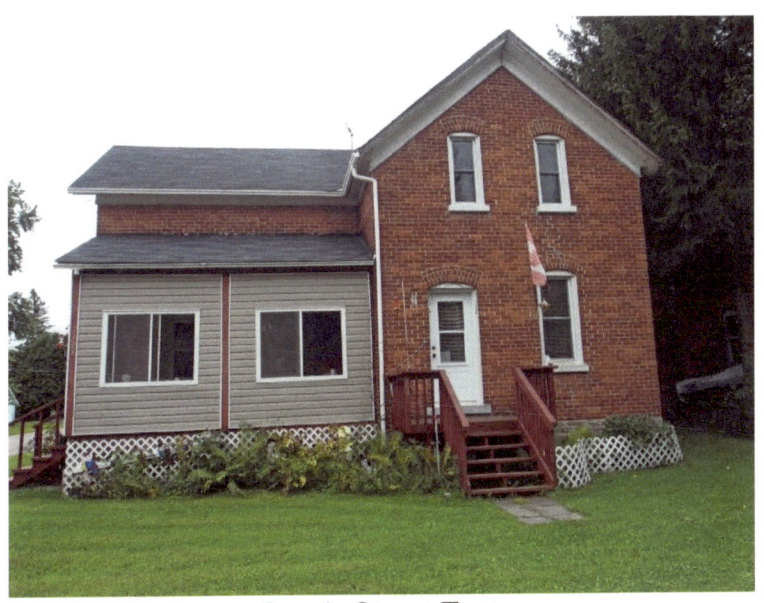

Lewis Street East

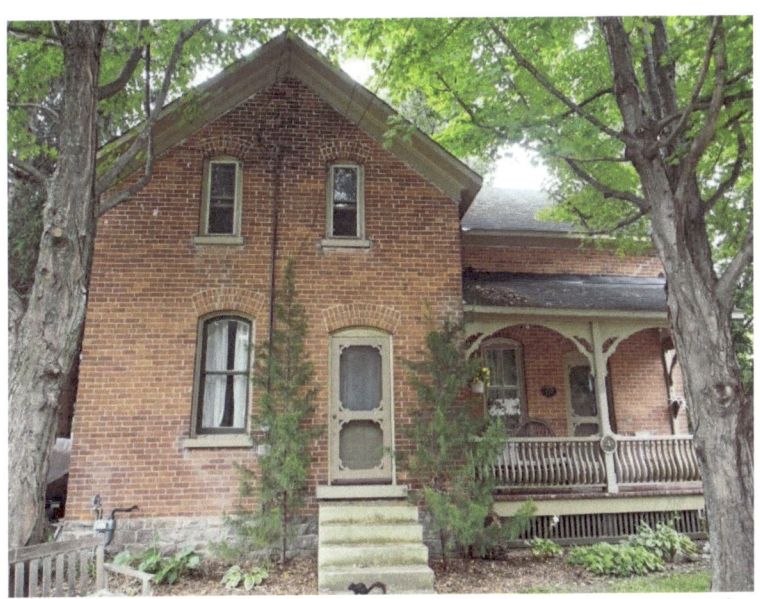

212 Lewis Street East - supports with decorative capitals on veranda, open railing

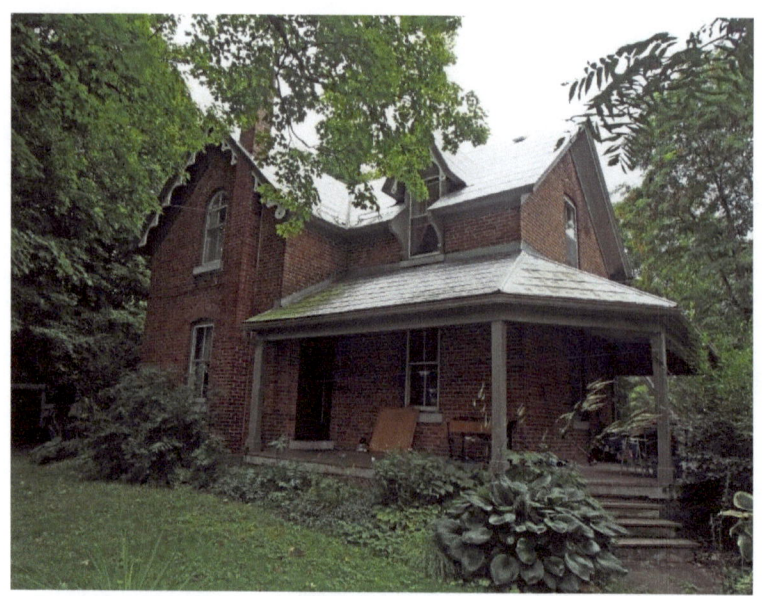

St. John Street – c. 1860 - verge board trim on gable

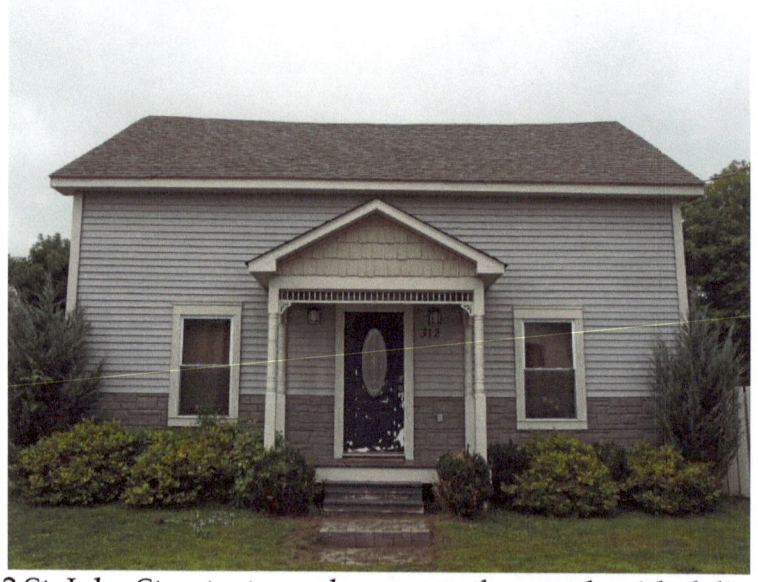

312 St. John Street – turned supports for porch with delicate spindles below pediment

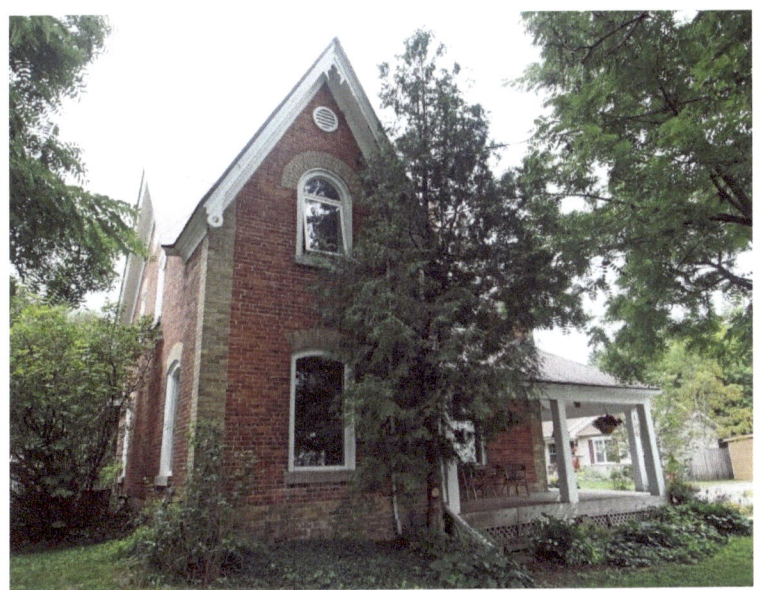

406 St. John Street – verge board trim on gable

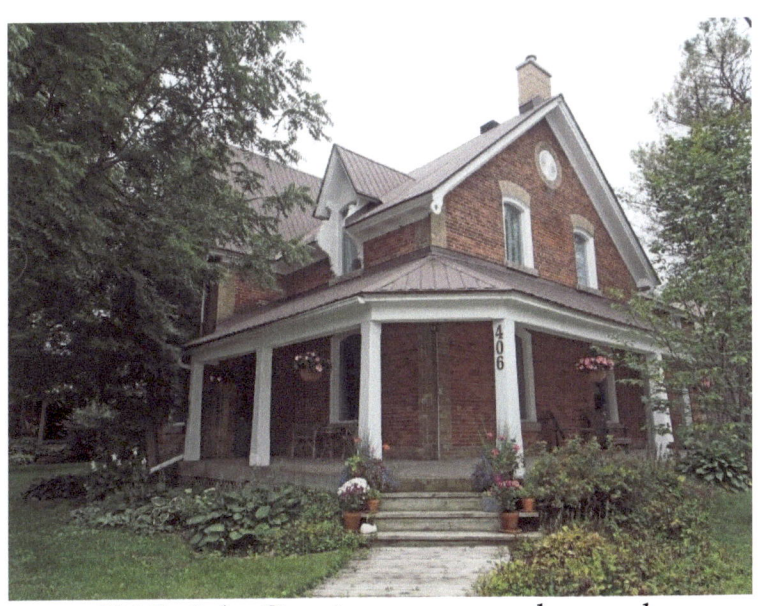

206 St. John Street – wraparound veranda

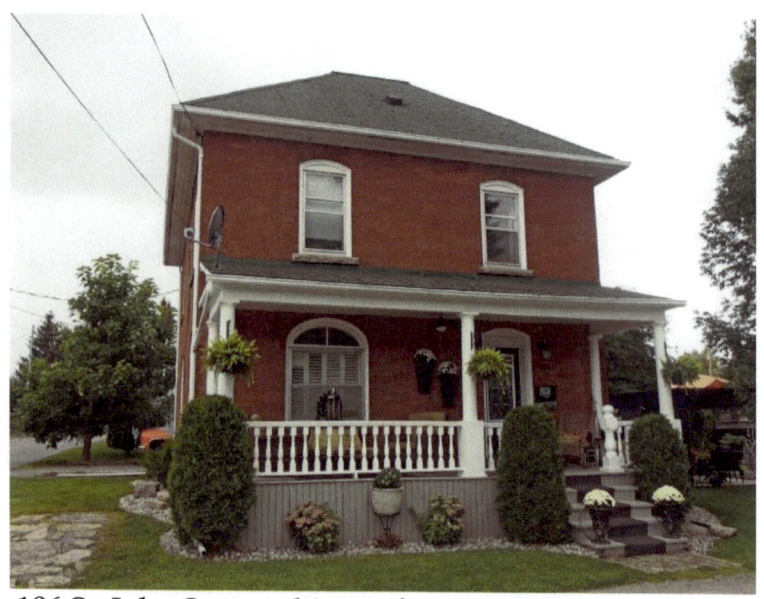

106 St. John Street – hip roof, open railing on veranda

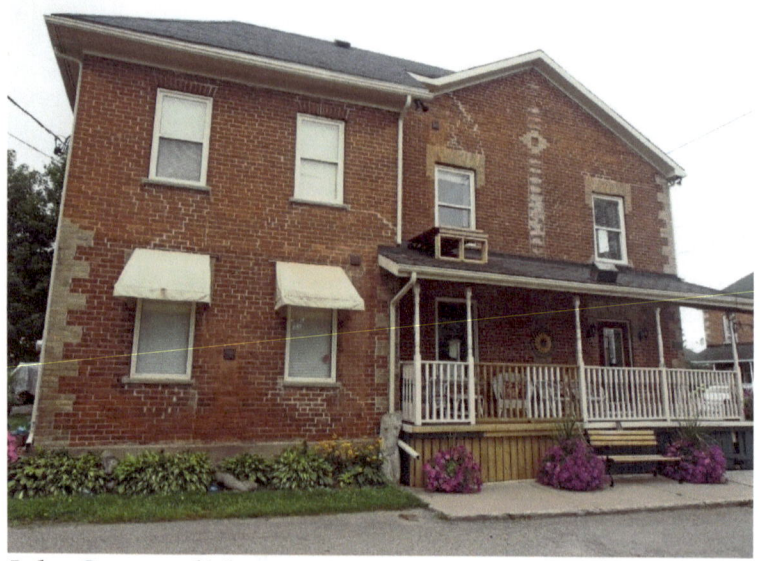

St. John Street - dichromatic voussoirs and quoins and other brickwork, open railing on veranda

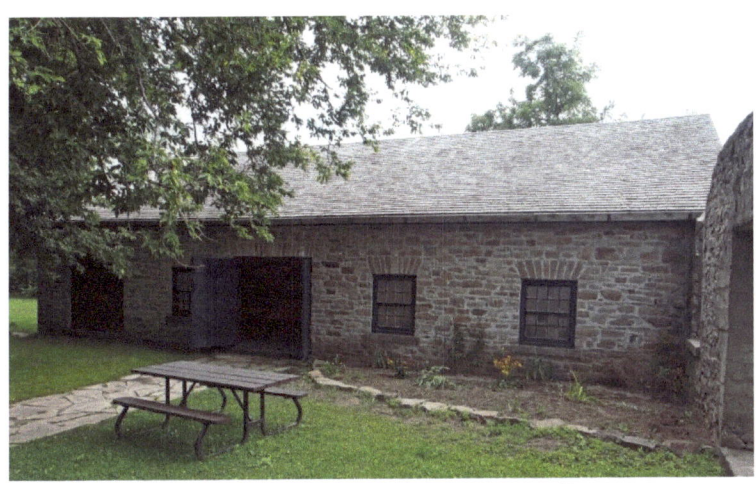

Merrickville Ruins Interpretive Center

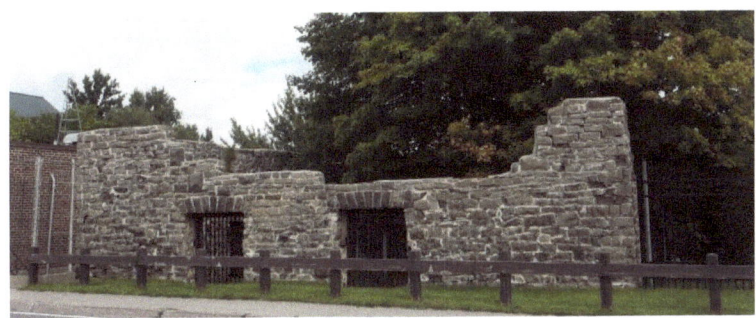

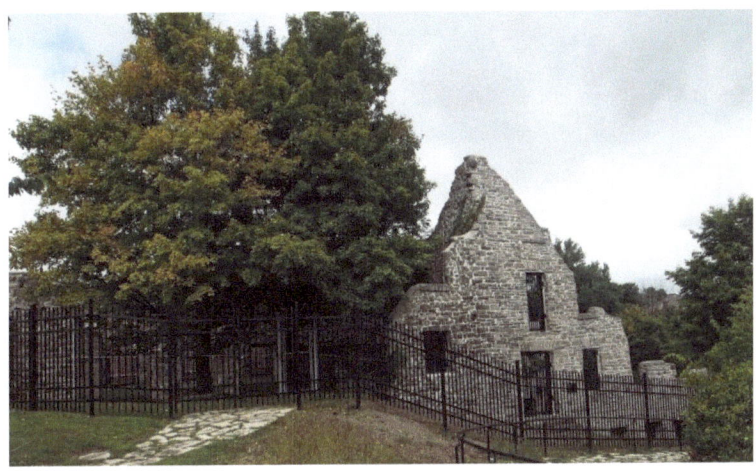

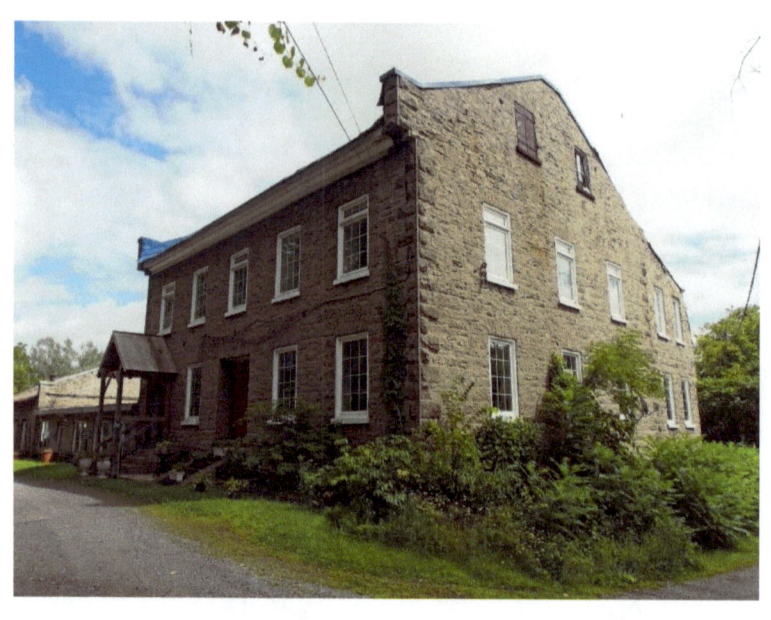

Industrial Complex – 1793

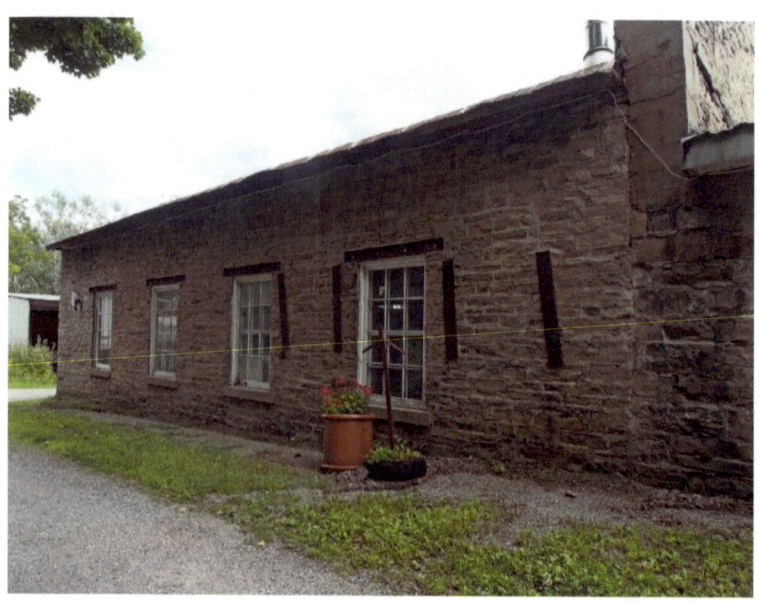

Architectural Terms

Bay Window: A window that projects out from a wall, in a semicircular, rectangular, or polygonal design. Used frequently in Gothic and Victorian designs. Example: Elgin Street, Page 59	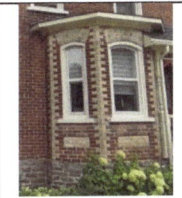
Brackets: a decorative or weight-bearing structural element which forms a right angle with one side against a wall and the other under a projecting surface such as an eave or roof. Example: 242 St. Lawrence Street, Page 24	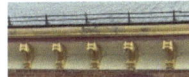
Buttress: a masonry structure built against or projecting from a wall which serves to support or reinforce the wall. In Canadian architecture, they are sometimes used for decoration. Example: 105 Church Street, Page 44	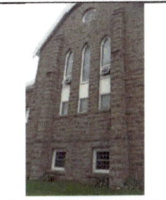
Capital: The uppermost finish or decoration on a column. An Ionic column has a small base, a thin elegant shaft, and a capital composed of volutes which are carved whirls or twists that take the form of a scroll. Example: 818 St. Lawrence Street, Page 7 A Doric column is characterized by a plain column with no base, a shaft with twenty flutings, and a simple capital with a simple entablature. Example: Mill Street, Page 46	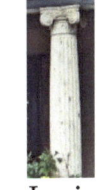 Ionic 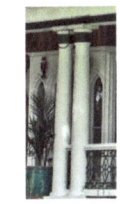 Doric
Cornice Return: decorative element on the end of a gable. Example: 305 Brock Street West, Page 52	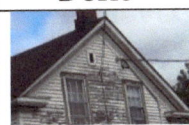

Course: continuous horizontal row or layer of stone or brick. Example: 612-606 St. Lawrence Street, Page 15	
Dentil Moulding: an even series of rectangles used as ornamental decoration in cornices. Example: 111 St. Lawrence Street, Page 26	
Dichromatic brickwork: the use of two colours of brick, tile or slate to decorate a façade. Example: St. John Street, Page 70	
Dormer: (French for "sleep") a gable end window that pierces through the plane of a sloping roof surface to create usable space in the top floor or attic of a building by adding headroom. Example: 905 St. Lawrence Street, Page 6	
Entrance: The entrance encompasses the doorway and the inner vestibule or, in residential architecture, the covered porch. Example: 136 Brock Street West, Page 50	
Fretwork: interlaced decorative design resembling a bracket Example: 223 Main Street East, Page 43	
Gable: the triangular portion of a wall between the edges of a sloping roof. **Jacobean Gable:** the gable extends above the roofline. Example: 211 St. Lawrence Street, Page 28	

Hipped Roof: a roof where all sides slope downwards to the walls with no gables. Example: 511 St. Lawrence Street, Page 18	
Keystones and Voussoirs: a voussoir is a wedge-shaped element used in building an arch. A keystone is the central stone that locks all the stones into position, allowing the arch to bear weight. A keystone is often enlarged and embellished. Example: Main Street West, Page 32	
Lancet Window: a tall, narrow window with a pointed arch at its top. Example: 618 St. Lawrence Street, Page 13	
Mansard Roof: This style was popularized by Francois Mansart (1598-1666), an accomplished architect of the French Baroque period and especially fashionable during the Second French Empire (1852-1870). This roof is almost flat on the top section, with two slopes on each of its sides with the lower slope at a steeper angle than the upper and having dormer windows. Example: 529 St. Lawrence Street, Page 16	
Palladian Window: a large window that is divided into three sections with the centre section larger than the two side sections and usually arched. Example: 205 Main Street West, Page 35	
Pediment: a triangular section above the door or portico, usually supported by columns. The inside of the triangle is called the tympanum. Example: 905 St. Lawrence Street, Page 6	

Pilaster: a slightly projecting column built into or applied to the face of a wall for additional structural support. Example: 111 St. Lawrence Street, Page 26	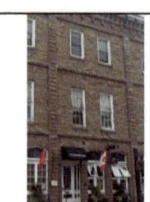
Quoin: masonry blocks at the corner of a wall, often a decorative feature, usually larger or of a different colour than the rest of the wall. Example: 612-606 St. Lawrence Street, Page 15	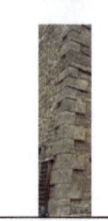
Rose Window: a circular window with ornamental tracery radiating from the centre. Example: 100 St. Lawrence Street, Page 31	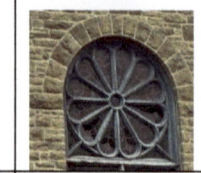
Sidelight: a vertical window that flanks a door, and is often used to emphasize the importance of a primary entrance. **Transom Window:** the light above the doorway, also called a fanlight. Example: 905 St. Lawrence Street, Page 6	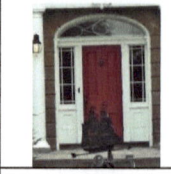
Tower: A circular, square, or octagonal vertical structure higher than the surrounding structure that is usually part of an existing building and is created either for extra defense or for a specific purpose such as a clock or a bell tower. Example: 205 Main Street West, Page 35	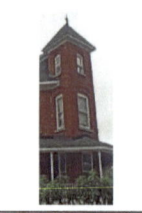
Verge board and Finial: hang from the projecting end of a roof and are often elaborately carved and ornamented. **Finial:** ornament added to the top of a gable, pinnacle, canopy or spire – a Gothic element. Example: 312 St. Lawrence Street, Page 24	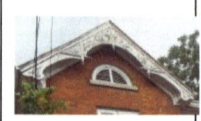

Building Styles

Edwardian, 1900-1930 – This style bridges the ornate and elaborate styles of the Victorian era and the simplified styles of the 20th century. Balanced facades, simple roof lines, dormer windows, large front porches, and smooth brick surfaces are its characteristics. Example: 523 St. Lawrence Street, Page 17	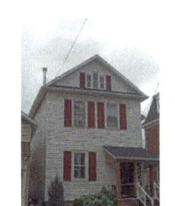
Gothic Revival, 1830-1890 – These decorative buildings have sharply-pitched gables with highly detailed verge boards, pointed-arch window openings, and dichromatic brickwork. It is a common style in Ontario. Example: 406 St. Lawrence Street, Page 21	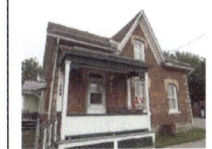
A **log cabin**, built from logs, usually one- or 1½-storeys constructed with round rather than hewn, or hand-worked, logs, and erected quickly for frontier shelter. Log cabins were built from logs laid horizontally and interlocked on the ends with notches. The cabin was situated to provide sunlight and drainage so the pioneers could cope better with the rigors of frontier life. The pioneers chose old-growth trees that were straight and had few knots and did not need to be hewn to fit well together. Careful notching minimized the size of the gap between the logs and reduced the amount of chinking with sticks and rocks or daubing with mud to fill the gap. The length of one log was the length of one wall. Example: 225 Brock Street West, Page 52	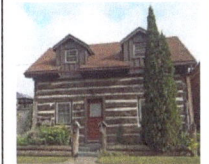

Neo-Classical, 1810-1850 – This style was a direct result of the War of 1812. Both residential and commercial buildings were constructed on the traditional Georgian plan, but they had a new gaiety and light-heartedness. Detailing became more refined, delicate, and elegant. Example: 905 St. Lawrence Street, Page 6	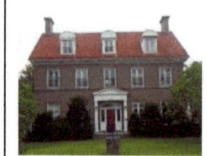
Queen Anne, 1885-1900 – an irregular outline featuring a combination of an offset tower, broad gables, projecting two-storey bays, verandahs, multi-sloped roofs, and tall, decorative chimneys. Example: 205 Main Street West, Page 35	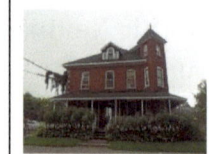
Regency Cottage, 1830-1860 – This style originated in England in 1815 and spread to Ontario later in the 19th century as British officers retired to Canada. It is a modest one-storey house with a low-pitched hip roof and has a symmetrical front façade. Example: 223 Main Street West, Page 33	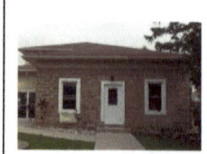
Romanesque Revival, 1880-1910 – This style hearkens back to medieval architecture of the 11th and 12th centuries with a heavy appearance, blocky towers and rounded arches. Example: 206 Main Street East, Page 41	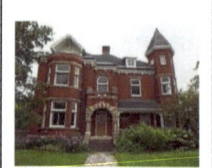
Second Empire, 1860-1880 – The mansard roof is the most noteworthy feature of this style and is evidence of the French origins. Projecting central towers and one or two-storey bays can also be present. Example: 317 St. Lawrence Street, Page 22	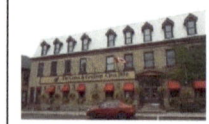

www.ingramcontent.com/pod-product-compliance
Lightning Source LLC
Chambersburg PA
CBHW040810200526
45159CB00022B/155